THE CLOUD COOK BOOK : RECIPES FOR CLOUD SUCCESS

A.DEVENDHIRAN

Contents

CHAPTER ONE

INTRODUCTION

The rapid expansion of cloud computing has transformed the way businesses operate, offering unprecedented scalability, flexibility, and cost-efficiency. However, harnessing the full potential of the cloud requires a strategic approach and a deep understanding of its complexities. This paper aims to delve into the intricacies of cloud computing, exploring its key components, benefits, challenges, and best practices for successful implementation. By examining real-world case studies and expert insights, this exploration seeks to provide a comprehensive overview of cloud computing and its transformative impact on contemporary organizations.

Recipes for Cloud Success is your comprehensive guide to navigating the dynamic landscape of cloud computing. From foundational concepts to advanced strategies, this book equips you with the knowledge and tools to architect, deploy, and optimize cloud-based solutions. Whether you're a cloud novice or a seasoned professional, you'll find practical insights, real-world examples, and expert advice to help you achieve your cloud goals. Discover how to leverage cloud computing to drive innovation, enhance efficiency, and gain a competitive edge in today's digital era. Cloud computing has revolutionized the IT landscape, offering unparalleled scalability, flexibility, and cost-effectiveness. However, navigating the complexities of cloud adoption and optimization requires a strategic approach. This paper aims to provide a comprehensive overview of cloud computing, exploring its fundamental concepts, key benefits, and potential challenges. By examining various cloud deployment models, service models, and emerging trends, this analysis seeks to equip readers with the knowledge necessary to harness the full potential of cloud technology and drive digital transformation within their organizations.

Forget the days of lugging around hefty laptops and worrying about running out of storage space. Cloudbooks are revolutionizing the way we compute, offering a refreshingly light and user-friendly experience. These sleek devices prioritize cloud storage and web-based applications, making them ideal for anyone who values portability and affordability. Unlike traditional laptops that rely on internal hard drives, cloudbooks leverage the power of the internet, allowing you to access your files, documents, and applications from anywhere with a stable connection. This eliminates the need for bulky local storage and the constant fear of data loss due to hardware failure. Furthermore, cloudbooks typically run on streamlined operating systems, requiring less processing power and resulting in extended battery life. This makes them perfect for students, travelers, or anyone who needs a reliable on-the-go companion for browsing the web, managing emails, working on documents, or even enjoying multimedia content. Whether you're a casual user or someone who needs a device for basic productivity tasks, cloudbooks offer a compelling alternative to traditional laptops, providing a seamless and cost-effective way to stay connected and productive in today's digital world. Forget lugging around hefty laptops and worrying about overflowing hard drives. Cloudbooks, a revolutionary breed of computers, are ushering in a new era of streamlined computing focused on the power of the internet. These lightweight devices prioritize cloud storage and web-based applications, offering a refreshingly portable and budget-friendly solution for your everyday needs. Whether you're a student juggling assignments, a professional managing emails and documents, or simply someone who enjoys browsing and entertainment, a cloudbook can be your perfect companion. They boast a compact design, making them ideal for slipping into your backpack or carrying around on the go. But don't be fooled by their size – cloudbooks are surprisingly powerful when it comes to everyday tasks. Because they rely on cloud storage and web apps, you won't be bogged down by bulky operating systems or limited internal storage. This also means you can access your files and applications from any device with an internet connection, offering incredible flexibility and peace of mind. So, if you're looking for a reliable, portable, and affordable way to stay connected and productive, then a cloudbook might just be the perfect fit for you.

CHAPTER TWO

CLOUD INGREDIENTS

Forget the days of complex cookbooks filled with cryptic instructions and unfamiliar ingredients. The cloud is revolutionizing how we approach technology, offering a refreshing and accessible solution for businesses and individuals alike. Just like in the kitchen, where delicious dishes are created with the right combination of ingredients and techniques, navigating the cloud requires a core set of components to achieve success. This book, titled "The Cloud Cookbook: Recipes for Cloud Success," serves as your culinary guide to the cloud, providing you with all the essential ingredients and step-by-step recipes to build secure, scalable, and cost-effective cloud solutions. Whether you're a seasoned IT professional or a curious newcomer, this book is designed to empower you on your cloud journey. We'll explore the fundamental ingredients – the cloud providers, storage options, compute services, and networking tools – that form the foundation of your cloud kitchen. We'll delve into the art of infrastructure as code (IaC), the secret ingredient that ensures consistent and repeatable deployments. We'll then explore various methods for deploying applications, from containerization with Docker and Kubernetes to the magic of serverless computing. But a successful cloud kitchen isn't just about preparing dishes; it's about keeping an eye on them. We'll equip you with cloud monitoring tools to ensure your applications are performing optimally, and delve into cost optimization strategies to help you manage your cloud spending efficiently. Security is paramount, so we'll explore essential measures to safeguard your data and resources. And just like any good chef prepares for unexpected situations, we'll guide you through disaster recovery best practices to ensure your cloud kitchen can weather any storm. As you progress through this book, you'll gain the confidence to explore advanced cloud techniques like serverless databases, machine learning, and artificial intelligence services, allowing you to create truly exquisite cloud solutions. So, grab your apron, preheat your metaphorical oven, and get ready to embark on a delicious journey into the world of cloud computing!

UNDERSTANDING CLOUD COMPONENTS

The cloud, like a well-stocked kitchen, is brimming with essential ingredients that combine to create powerful and scalable solutions. Just as a chef wouldn't attempt a complex dish without understanding their tools, mastering the cloud requires a firm grasp of its core components. This chapter dives deep into these fundamental building blocks, equipping you with the knowledge to navigate the cloud like a seasoned professional.

The Cloud Provider:

The cloud provider serves as the foundation of your cloud kitchen. These companies, like

- Amazon Web Services (AWS)
- Microsoft Azure
- Google Cloud Platform (GCP)

offer a vast array of services and resources that you can leverage to build your cloud infrastructure. Choosing the right provider depends on your specific needs, budget, and familiarity with their platforms. Each provider offers a unique set of features, pricing structures, and geographic reach. Consider factors like scalability, security offerings, available services, and customer support when making your selection.

Storage Options:

Just like a kitchen needs a well-stocked pantry and fridge, the cloud offers various storage options to hold your data.

- **Object Storage:** This is your virtual catch-all, ideal for storing large, unstructured data like backups, logs, and media files. It's highly scalable and cost-effective.
- **Block Storage:** Imagine this as your digital hard drive, perfect for storing structured data like databases and applications. It offers predictable performance and is ideal for frequently accessed data.
- **File Storage:** This functions like a cloud-based filing cabinet, allowing you to organize and share files easily with collaborators.

Compute Services: Workhorses

The cloud kitchen wouldn't function without ovens and stoves. Similarly, compute services are the workhorses of cloud environment. They provide the processing power and resources needed to run your applications. Here are the main types:

Virtual Machines (VMs): These are virtual computers that provide a dedicated environment with an operating system and resources. They offer flexibility but require more management overhead.

Containers: Think of containers as modular kitchens prepped for specific tasks. They offer faster deployment and lighter resource footprints than VMs. Technologies like Docker and Kubernetes simplify containerized application management.

Serverless Computing: This is like having a team of sous chefs handle specific tasks on demand. You simply define the functionality, and the cloud provider manages the underlying infrastructure. Serverless computing is ideal for event-driven applications and eliminates the need to manage servers.

Networking: Connecting Your Kitchen

- A well-connected kitchen ensures ingredients and dishes move smoothly.
- Cloud networking provides the virtual infrastructure that allows communication between different resources within your cloud environment and with the outside world.
- This includes virtual switches, routers, firewalls, and load balancers, all working together to create a secure and efficient network.

Understanding These Components is Just the Beginning

By grasping these essential cloud components, laid the groundwork for building robust and scalable cloud solutions. This chapter serves as your initial foray into the cloud kitchen. As you progress through this book, deeper into each component, exploring advanced features, configuration options, and best practices for leveraging them in various cloud recipes.

CHOOSING THE RIGHT CLOUD PROVIDER

Selecting the right cloud provider is akin to picking the perfect ingredients for your culinary masterpiece. Just as different spices and herbs enhance a dish in unique ways, each cloud provider offers its own set of features and functionalities. Understanding these options equips you to make an informed decision that aligns with your specific needs and preferences. Let's delve deeper into the factors to consider when choosing your cloud provider.

A Look at Cloud Provider Services

Cloud providers offer a diverse range of services, forming the core ingredients of your cloud kitchen. Here's a closer look at some key offerings:

Compute Services: As mentioned earlier, these services provide the processing power to run your applications. Options like virtual machines, containers, and serverless computing cater to various needs.

Storage Options: From object storage for large datasets to block storage for databases and file storage for collaboration, cloud providers offer a variety of storage solutions.

- Object storage: Holds large, unstructured data (backups, logs, media) – think bulk ingredients.
- Block storage: Ideal for structured data like databases (think pre-cut ingredients).
- File storage: Organizes and shares files for collaboration (think your digital recipe box).

Networking Services: These services ensure smooth communication within your cloud environment and with the internet. They include virtual networks, firewalls, load balancers, and other tools.

- Virtual networks: These create dedicated communication channels for your cloud resources.
- Firewalls: Act as security guards, controlling incoming and outgoing traffic.
- Load balancers: Distribute traffic across multiple resources, ensuring smooth operation during peak hours.

Database Services: Cloud providers offer managed database solutions for various needs, eliminating the need for self-management and scaling headaches. Database services are like pre-built kitchen appliances for your cloud. Cloud providers offer various managed solutions, saving you time and effort:

- You don't have to worry about manually installing, configuring, or scaling your databases.
- They handle maintenance and updates, freeing you to focus on your applications.
- You have access to a wider range of database options, allowing you to choose the best fit for your needs.

Analytics and Machine Learning: Many providers offer pre-built tools and services for data analytics and machine learning, allowing you to extract insights from your data and build intelligent applications. Cloud providers offer data analysis and machine learning (ML) like a well-stocked spice rack for your culinary creations:

- Pre-built tools simplify data analysis, letting you extract valuable insights from your information.
- ML services act like secret ingredients, enabling you to build intelligent applications without being an ML

expert

Security Services: Cloud providers offer robust security features like access control, encryption, and identity management to safeguard your data and resources. Cloud security is the vault in your cloud kitchen, keeping your ingredients (data) safe. Providers offer features like:

- Access control: Locks on the pantry, restricting who can access your resources.
- Encryption: Keeps your recipes secret, even if someone peeks in the vault.
- Identity management: Ensures only authorized chefs can enter the kitchen.

Matching Flavors to Your Palate: Considering Your Needs

The ideal cloud provider is not a one-size-fits-all solution. Here are some crucial questions to ask yourself when evaluating options:

- Application Requirements:Consider the processing power, storage needs, and scalability requirements of your applications.

- Security and Compliance: What are your security needs? Does the provider offer features that comply with relevant industry regulations?
- Scalability: How will your needs grow over time? Choose a provider that offers flexible scaling options to accommodate your future growth.
- Cost and Pricing: Cloud providers have different pricing models. Consider the pay-as-you-go approach offered

by most providers and explore features like reserved instances or spot instances to optimize your cloud spending.

- Geographic Reach: Where do you need your cloud resources to be located? Choose a provider with a global presence if geographic distribution is important.
- Support and Customer Service: Evaluate the level of support offered by the provider. Do they offer 24/7 support, and are there different tiers available?

Comparing Major Cloud Providers

The three main players in the cloud computing market are:

Amazon Web Services (AWS): The industry leader, AWS offers a vast array of services, making it a versatile choice for diverse needs. However, its complexity may be overwhelming for beginners.

Microsoft Azure: Azure is known for its tight integration with Microsoft products and services. It caters well to enterprise-level needs and offers strong security features.

Google Cloud Platform (GCP): Known for its innovative technologies and competitive pricing, GCP is a strong contender for data analytics and machine learning workloads.

Tasting the Options: Free Trials and Experimentation

Many cloud providers offer free trials that allow you to explore their services and evaluate their suitability for your needs. Take advantage of these trials to get hands-on experience and find the provider that best suits your palate.

Choosing the right cloud provider is a crucial first step in your cloud journey. By understanding the "spice rack" of cloud services offered by different providers, carefully considering your needs, and exploring various options, you can select a partner that helps you create delicious (and successful) cloud solutions.

ESSENTIAL CLOUD SERVICES

The cloud, much like a well-equipped kitchen, relies on a set of essential services to function effectively. These services act as your core ingredients, providing the foundation for building secure, scalable, and cost-efficient cloud solutions. Let's delve deeper into the three fundamental categories of cloud services and explore the functionalities they offer:

1. Compute Services:

The Workhorses of Your Cloud Kitchen-

Compute services are the engines that power your cloud environment. They provide the processing power and resources needed to run your applications, databases, and other workloads. Here's a breakdown of the key players:

Virtual Machines (VMs)

Imagine these as virtual computers in the cloud. They offer a dedicated environment with an operating system and resources, similar to a physical computer. VMs provide a familiar and flexible environment for running various applications. However, they require more management overhead compared to other options.

Containers

Think of containers as modular kitchens prepped for specific tasks. Unlike VMs, containers share the operating system kernel with other containers on the same host machine. This makes them lightweight, portable, and faster to deploy than VMs. Technologies like Docker and Kubernetes simplify containerized application management and orchestration.

Serverless Computing

This innovative approach removes server management from the equation. With serverless computing, you simply define the functionality needed, and the cloud provider manages the underlying infrastructure that executes your code. This is ideal for event-driven applications or tasks that require short bursts of processing power.

Choosing the Right Compute Service:

- Consider your application requirements: What resources (CPU, memory) does your application need? Does it require a dedicated environment (VM) or the flexibility of containers?
- Scalability: How will your needs grow over time? VMs offer flexibility in scaling resources, while serverless computing scales automatically based on demand.
- Management Overhead: Are you comfortable managing server infrastructure (VMs) or do you prefer a hands-off approach (serverless)?

2. Storage Options:

The Pantry and Fridge of Your Cloud Kitchen-

Just as a kitchen needs dedicated spaces for different types of ingredients, cloud storage comes in various flavors to accommodate diverse data needs:

Object Storage

Think of this as your virtual catch-all, ideal for storing large, unstructured data like backups, logs, and media files. Object storage is highly scalable and cost-effective, making it perfect for archiving or infrequently accessed data.

Block Storage

Imagine this as your digital hard drive. Block storage provides reliable and predictable performance, making it ideal for storing structured data like databases and applications that require frequent access.

File Storage

This functions like a cloud-based filing cabinet, allowing you to organize and share files easily with collaborators. It offers a user-friendly interface for accessing and managing your files.

Choosing the Right Storage Option:

- Data Type: What type of data are you storing? Unstructured data (backups) goes well with object storage, while structured data (databases) benefits from block storage.
- Performance Needs: Do you require fast access and read/write capabilities (block storage) or is cost-efficiency a bigger priority (object storage)?
- Sharing Needs: Do you need to collaborate on files (file storage) or is individual access sufficient (object/block storage)?

3. Networking Services:

The Invisible Waiters Ensuring Smooth Operations-

Networking services are the behind-the-scenes heroes that ensure seamless communication within your cloud environment and with the outside world. These services function like the invisible waiters in a restaurant, facilitating data flow and ensuring smooth operation:

Virtual Networks (VPCs)

These create dedicated communication channels within your cloud environment. Think of them as private networks within the broader cloud infrastructure, allowing resources to communicate securely without being exposed to the public internet.

Firewalls

Act as security guards, controlling incoming and outgoing traffic. Firewalls filter traffic based on predefined rules, ensuring only authorized traffic enters and exits your VPC.

Load Balancers

Imagine a restaurant with a long line – load balancers distribute traffic across multiple resources (servers) to prevent overloading and ensure smooth performance during peak times.

Content Delivery Networks (CDNs)

These geographically distributed networks deliver content (websites, applications) to users with minimal latency. Think of them as regional kitchens strategically placed to serve customers quickly.

Choosing the Right Networking Service:

- Security Needs: Firewalls are essential for controlling access and protecting your resources.
- Scalability: Load balancers ensure smooth operation during traffic spikes.
- Performance: CDNs improve website and application performance for geographically dispersed users.

By understanding these essential cloud services and their functionalities, you'll be well-equipped to select the right tools for your specific needs. Remember, the cloud kitchen analogy can guide

Infrastructure as a Service (IaaS), Platform as a Service (PaaS), Software as a Service (SaaS)

Imagine a cloud computing service as a restaurant serving up solutions for your business needs. Here's how Infrastructure as a Service (IaaS), Platform as a Service (PaaS), and Software as a Service (SaaS) translate into distinct dining experiences:

IaaS: The Solid Platforms

Analogy: IaaS is like a bring-your-own-groceries restaurant. You rent the kitchen space (computing resources like servers, storage, and networking) but bring your own ingredients (operating systems, applications, and data).

Control and Flexibility: You have maximum control over your infrastructure, similar to having complete control over your recipe and cooking methods in the kitchen you rent.

Responsibility: Just like you're responsible for buying groceries and cooking the meal, you manage everything from operating systems to security in IaaS.

Businesses requiring granular control over their infrastructure for specific needs, like running custom applications or managing sensitive data.

PaaS: The Pre-Built Kitchen

Analogy: PaaS is like a restaurant offering a partially prepared meal. You get a pre-configured platform (operating system, development tools, databases) to build and deploy your applications, but you still manage the ingredients (your application code and data).

Efficiency and Development Focus: Saves time on setting up the underlying infrastructure, allowing you to focus on application development, similar to how a pre-built kitchen streamlines prep work for chefs.

Scalability: PaaS platforms often offer easy scaling options, letting you adjust resources as your application needs grow. Think of it as having a kitchen that can expand to accommodate more orders during peak hours.

Businesses that want to develop and deploy applications quickly without managing the complexities of the underlying infrastructure.

SaaS: The Complete Package

Analogy: SaaS is like a full-service restaurant where you're served a ready-to-eat meal. The provider takes care of everything – the infrastructure, platform, application, and data management. You simply log in and use the service.

Simplicity and Ease of Use: Requires minimal setup or maintenance, similar to how you don't need to worry about cooking or cleaning at a full-service restaurant.

Cost-Effectiveness: Can be a cost-effective option for basic needs, especially for smaller businesses or for specific applications. Think of it as a budget-friendly option compared to building and maintaining your own infrastructure.

Limited Customization: Offers less customization compared to IaaS or PaaS, just like a restaurant meal might not cater to all dietary preferences.

Choosing the Right Service:

The best cloud computing service depends on your specific needs:

- For maximum control and customization: Choose IaaS.
- For a balance between control and development speed: Choose PaaS.
- For simplicity and ease of use: Choose SaaS.

Cloud computing offers a variety of options to cater to your specific business needs. By understanding the IaaS, PaaS, and SaaS models – like navigating a diverse restaurant menu – you can choose the service that provides the right ingredients and cooking environment for your digital success.

CHAPTER THREE

CLOUD RECIPES

The cloud is your playground, and this book is your ultimate guide to becoming a cloud champion. Imagine conquering challenges, earning badges, and unlocking new levels as you master essential cloud concepts. That's the power of gamified learning, and this book, "The Cloud Cookbook: Recipes for Cloud Success," uses this innovative approach to transform your cloud journey into an exciting adventure. This book equips you with the basic gear understanding cloud providers, storage options, compute services, and networking fundamentals. Think of them as your starter quests, providing a solid foundation for building your cloud expertise. The art of infrastructure as code (IaC), the secret weapon that allows you to automate deployments with precision and speed. Consider these advanced quests that unlock the power of consistency and efficiency. We'll then explore various deployment strategies, from containerization to serverless computing, giving you a diverse toolkit to tackle problems with the perfect "cloud recipe." But a successful cloud champion doesn't just build; they monitor and optimize. We'll equip you with cloud monitoring tools, akin to performance trackers in the game, allowing you to keep a watchful eye on your applications and ensure they're running smoothly.

We'll also delve into cost optimization strategies, teaching you how to manage your cloud resources like a pro, maximizing value and avoiding unnecessary spending. Security is the ultimate boss battle in the cloud game. We'll provide you with the knowledge and tools to defend your cloud environment like a seasoned warrior. Learn about access control, encryption, and disaster recovery best practices – the ultimate shields and armor to protect your data and applications from any threat. These badges are more than just bragging rights; they represent your mastery of essential cloud skills. More importantly, you'll gain the confidence to explore advanced cloud techniques like serverless databases, machine learning, and artificial intelligence, allowing you to create truly groundbreaking cloud solutions. So, grab your controller and prepare to level up your cloud skills.

APPETIZERS- QUICK CLOUD DEPLOYMENTS

The cloud offers incredible agility and scalability, but sometimes you need to get your applications up and running even faster. That's where quick cloud deployments come in – a set of techniques and tools that allow you to provision and configure your cloud environment in a matter of minutes, not hours or days. Here's a breakdown of some key methods for achieving lightning-fast cloud deployments:

1. Infrastructure as Code (IaC):

IaC is the game-changer for quick deployments. Imagine writing code that defines your entire cloud infrastructure – servers, networks, storage – instead of manually configuring everything through a web console. This code can be version controlled, shared, and reused, ensuring consistent and repeatable deployments every time. Popular IaC tools like Terraform and AWS CloudFormation allow you to automate infrastructure provisioning, saving you hours of manual configuration.

2. Pre-built Templates:

Many cloud providers offer pre-built infrastructure templates for common use cases – web servers, databases, development environments. These templates act as pre-configured starter packs, allowing you to quickly deploy basic infrastructure with minimal configuration. Think of them as pre-made meals in the cloud kitchen – they save you time chopping vegetables (configuring resources) and allow you to focus on the unique elements of your application.

3. Containerization:

Containers, like Docker containers, package your application and its dependencies into a lightweight, self-contained unit. This allows for rapid deployment across different environments, including the cloud. Containers are quick to start and stop, making them ideal for microservices architectures and rapid experimentation. Imagine pre-assembled meals (containers) with all the ingredients (code and dependencies) ready to be cooked (deployed) in any cloud kitchen (environment).

4. Serverless Computing:

Serverless computing takes the concept of quick deployments to a whole new level. With serverless, you simply focus on writing the code for your application logic, and the cloud provider handles all the underlying infrastructure. This eliminates the need for provisioning, managing, and scaling servers, allowing for near-instantaneous deployments. Think of it as ordering pre-cooked meals (serverless functions) delivered straight to your table (cloud environment) – all you need to do is heat them up (execute the code).

5. Infrastructure as Service (IaaS) Marketplaces:

Many cloud providers offer IaaS marketplaces with pre-configured software packages and appliances. These marketplaces are like virtual grocery stores filled with pre-made ingredients (pre-configured software). You can find everything from databases and development tools to security solutions and monitoring tools, all ready to be deployed in your cloud environment with just a few clicks.

By leveraging these techniques, you can significantly reduce the time it takes to deploy your applications in the cloud. This allows for faster iteration, quicker time-to-market, and the ability to respond to changing business needs with greater agility. So, the next time you need to get your cloud project up and running in a hurry, remember these quick deployment strategies and watch your cloud kitchen come to life in record time.

MAIN COURSE- BUILDINGS SCALABLE CLOUD APPLICATION

The beauty of the cloud lies in its ability to adapt and grow alongside your business. Unlike traditional IT infrastructure, cloud resources can be scaled up or down on demand, ensuring your applications can handle fluctuating user traffic and evolving business needs. This chapter dives into the essential principles and techniques for crafting scalable cloud applications:

Design for Scalability:

The foundation of a scalable application is a well-thought-out architecture. Don't be fooled by the initial simplicity of your project – consider how it might need to grow in the future. Here are some key principles to keep in mind:

Microservices Architecture: Break down your application into smaller, independent services that communicate with each other via APIs. This modular approach allows you to scale individual services independently based on their specific needs. Imagine building your application with pre-prepared ingredients (microservices) that can be easily added or removed to adjust portion sizes (application capacity).

Stateless Design: Strive to make your application components stateless. This means they don't store data on their own and rely on external data sources like databases. Stateless applications are easier to scale horizontally by adding more instances to handle increased load. Think of stateless components like short-order cooks who don't need to remember specific orders (data) – they simply prepare each request (user interaction) independently.

Horizontal Scaling: This involves adding more instances of your application components to distribute the workload. It's like adding more ovens to your cloud kitchen during peak hours to handle a surge in orders. Cloud providers make horizontal scaling a breeze, allowing you to add resources with minimal effort.

Leverage Cloud-Native Technologies:

Embrace the power of cloud-specific tools and services to build truly scalable applications:

Auto Scaling: This feature offered by most cloud providers automatically scales your resources (servers) up or down based on predefined metrics like CPU utilization. Think of it as a smart thermostat in your cloud kitchen – it automatically adjusts the heat (resources) based on the desired temperature (application performance).

Load Balancers: These distribute incoming traffic across multiple instances of your application, ensuring no single server gets overloaded. Imagine a restaurant with a dedicated greeter who directs customers (traffic) to available tables (application instances).

Embrace Monitoring and Observability:

Scalability requires constant vigilance. Implement cloud monitoring tools to track key performance indicators (KPIs) like response times and resource utilization. These tools act as diagnostics for your cloud kitchen, allowing you to identify bottlenecks and proactively address scalability issues. Additionally, observability tools provide deeper insights into application behavior, helping you understand how your application performs under different loads. Think of them as performance reviews for your chefs, allowing you to identify areas for improvement and optimize efficiency.

Design for Fault Tolerance:

Scalability isn't just about handling increased load; it's also about ensuring your application remains available even if some components fail. This is where fault tolerance comes in:

Redundancy: Deploy your application components across multiple availability zones within a region or even across different regions. This ensures that if one zone experiences an outage, your application can still function using resources in another zone. Imagine having multiple backup kitchens geographically dispersed to ensure service continuity even if one location faces issues.

Self-Healing Mechanisms: Implement mechanisms that automatically detect and recover from failures. This might involve restarting failed instances or rerouting traffic to healthy instances. Think of it as having a team of sous chefs ready to jump in and keep the kitchen running smoothly if a head chef (application component) encounters an issue.

These principles and leveraging the power of cloud-native technologies, you can build applications that are not only functional but also resilient and scalable. Remember, a scalable cloud application is like a well-designed recipe – it can be easily adapted to serve a small gathering or a large banquet, ensuring your cloud kitchen thrives under any circumstance.

DESSERTS:DATA-DRIVEN CLOUD INSIGHTS

Just like a skilled pastry chef uses data on ingredient ratios and baking times to create delectable desserts, data-driven insights are the secret ingredient for optimizing your cloud environment. In the cloud kitchen, data serves as your sugar and spice, providing valuable information to enhance performance, reduce costs, and ensure the long-term success of your cloud deployments. Let's explore the different flavors of data-driven cloud insights:

1.Performance Monitoring: The Sweet Satisfaction of Efficiency

Cloud monitoring tools collect a wealth of data about your application's performance in the cloud. Metrics like CPU utilization, memory usage, and response times offer a real-time view into how your applications are functioning. By analyzing this data, you can identify bottlenecks, diagnose issues, and optimize resource allocation. Imagine monitoring oven temperatures (CPU usage) and baking times (response times) to ensure your pastries bake perfectly (applications perform optimally).

2. Cost Optimization: Avoiding a Bitter Bill

Cloud billing can be a complex beast, but data-driven insights can help you avoid sticker shock. Cloud providers offer detailed cost breakdowns that show you exactly where your money is going. Analyze this data to identify underutilized resources or instances that can be scaled down. Spot unused ingredients (idle resources) in your cloud kitchen and adjust your recipe (resource allocation) to avoid waste (unnecessary spending).

3. User Behavior Insights: Understanding Your Customer's Palate

Many cloud applications generate data about user behavior. This data can be a goldmine for understanding your users' needs and preferences. Analyze user traffic patterns, clickstream data, and application logs to identify areas for improvement and personalize the user experience. Imagine studying customer feedback (usage data) to see which pastries are most popular and adjust your menu (application features) accordingly.

4. Security Monitoring: The Cherry on Top of Security

Cloud security is paramount, and data plays a crucial role in maintaining a safe environment. Security monitoring tools collect data on access attempts, suspicious activities, and potential vulnerabilities. By analyzing this data, you can identify and address security threats before they become major problems. Think of it as monitoring food safety protocols (security measures) and conducting regular inspections (data analysis) to ensure the hygiene (security) of your cloud kitchen.

5. Capacity Planning: Predicting Demand for Fresh Success

Cloud resources can be scaled up or down based on your needs. By analyzing historical data on user traffic and resource utilization, you can forecast future demand and proactively adjust your cloud infrastructure. Imagine studying seasonal sales trends (usage patterns) to stock up on the right ingredients (resources) before peak baking season (periods of high demand).

Data-driven insights are the secret ingredient that transforms your cloud deployments from good to great. By leveraging these "desserts" of valuable information, you can ensure your cloud kitchen operates efficiently, delivers a delightful user experience, and remains secure from any threats. So, embrace data as your culinary compass, analyze, optimize, and watch your cloud success story unfold.

BEVERAGES: CLOUD SECURITY AND COMPLIANCE

The beverage industry is experiencing a digital revolution. From smart manufacturing and automated supply chains to e-commerce platforms and personalized marketing, cloud computing is becoming an essential ingredient for success. However, this shift brings a new set of challenges: cloud security and compliance.

Cloud Security: Protecting the Secret Recipe

Cloud security ensures the confidentiality, integrity, and availability of a beverage company's data stored in the cloud. This includes:

- **Protecting sensitive information:** Formulas, trade secrets, and customer data (like purchase history or dietary restrictions) are all valuable assets that need robust protection against unauthorized access.
- **Securing infrastructure:** Cloud providers offer a vast infrastructure, but it's crucial to understand their security measures and implement additional controls, like encryption, to safeguard your specific needs.
- **Preventing cyberattacks:** The beverage industry is increasingly targeted for cyberattacks, aiming to disrupt operations, steal intellectual property, or manipulate production processes. Implementing robust security protocols and employee training are vital.

Compliance: Keeping it Safe and Legal

Compliance refers to adhering to industry regulations and data privacy laws. For beverage companies, this might involve:

- **Food safety regulations:** Many countries have strict regulations regarding food and beverage safety. Cloud-based systems must ensure data integrity for traceability and quality control.
- **Data privacy laws:** Consumer data like purchase history and dietary preferences must be protected according to regulations like GDPR (Europe) or CCPA (California). Cloud providers should offer features to comply with these regulations.
- **Industry-specific standards:** Certain beverage segments might have additional compliance requirements. For example, some countries require detailed ingredient tracking for allergen labelling. The cloud solution should be adaptable to these needs.

Finding the Right Blend

Balancing cloud security and compliance can be a complex task, but it's crucial for the beverage industry. Here are some tips:

1. **Choose a reputable cloud provider:** Select a provider known for strong security practices and compliance certifications relevant to your industry.
2. **Implement a comprehensive security strategy:** Develop a layered approach that includes data encryption, access controls, and regular vulnerability assessments.
3. **Train employees on cybersecurity:** Educate staff on cyber threats and best practices for secure data handling

in the cloud environment.

4. **Stay informed about compliance regulations:** Continuously monitor and adapt your cloud strategy to evolving regulations and industry standards.

By prioritizing cloud security and compliance, beverage companies can unlock the full potential of digital transformation while ensuring the safety, security, and privacy of their valuable data. Remember, in the world of cloud computing for beverages, a secure and compliant blend is the recipe for success.

CLOUD-NATIVE APPLICATION

In today's dynamic digital landscape, businesses are increasingly turning to cloud computing for agility, scalability, and efficiency. But simply migrating existing applications to the cloud isn't always enough to reap the full benefits. This is where cloud-native applications come in. Imagine them as the perfectly suited chefs for your cloud kitchen – designed and optimized to thrive in this digital environment.

Traditional Applications vs. Cloud-Native Applications:

Traditional Applications: Often monolithic, bulky software programs built for on-premise servers. They can be slow to adapt and struggle to scale effectively in the cloud. Imagine a traditional chef struggling to adapt their recipes and cooking methods to a completely new kitchen environment.

Cloud-Native Applications: Designed specifically for the cloud, built from the ground up with microservices architecture, containerization, and DevOps principles. Think of a cloud-native application as a team of specialized chefs collaborating seamlessly in a well-equipped cloud kitchen.

Key Characteristics of Cloud-Native Applications:

Microservices Architecture: Applications are broken down into smaller, independent, and loosely coupled services, each with a specific function. This allows for independent development, deployment, and scaling. Imagine each chef specializing in a particular dish, allowing for faster preparation and easier adaptation to changing customer demands.

Containerization: Microservices are packaged in containers, lightweight units that include all the dependencies needed to run the service on any cloud platform. This ensures portability and consistency across environments. Think of each container as a pre-measured and prepped set of ingredients for a specific dish, ready to be cooked in any cloud kitchen.

DevOps Principles: Cloud-native development embraces DevOps, a culture of collaboration between developers and operations teams. This fosters rapid development cycles, continuous integration and delivery (CI/CD), and automated infrastructure provisioning. Imagine the chefs and kitchen staff working together seamlessly, with streamlined processes for recipe creation, ingredient preparation, and order fulfillment.

Benefits of Cloud-Native Applications:

- Increased Agility: Microservices architecture allows for faster development, deployment, and updates. The cloud-native chefs can adapt their recipes and menus quickly based on customer feedback or changing market demands.
- Improved Scalability: Applications can easily scale up or down based on demand by scaling individual

microservices. The cloud kitchen can adjust its staffing and resource allocation based on the number of orders coming in.

- Enhanced Resilience: Failure in one microservice doesn't bring down the entire application. Other services can continue to function, similar to how a single dish being unavailable in the cloud kitchen wouldn't halt operations entirely.
- Higher Efficiency: Containerization and automation streamline deployment and resource management. The cloud kitchen utilizes its resources effectively, reducing waste and optimizing overall operational efficiency.

Cloud-native applications are the future of software development for the cloud era. By embracing this approach, businesses can unlock the full potential of cloud computing and gain a competitive edge in the digital marketplace. Just like a well-designed cloud kitchen delivers exceptional culinary experiences, cloud-native applications empower businesses to create innovative and scalable solutions that meet the ever-evolving demands of the digital world.

HYBRID CLOUD SOLUTION

Imagine a restaurant that offers both an à la carte menu and a daily special. This is the essence of a hybrid cloud solution: it combines the flexibility and scalability of the public cloud with the security and control of a private cloud, giving you the freedom to choose the perfect environment for each of your digital dishes.

Why Choose Hybrid Cloud?

Tailored Deployment: Not all applications have the same needs. A hybrid cloud lets you deploy security-sensitive applications on your private cloud, while resource-intensive workloads can leverage the scalability of the public cloud. It's like offering both gourmet dishes prepared in your own kitchen (private cloud) and crowd-pleasing favorites sourced from a reliable supplier (public cloud).

Flexibility and Control: Hybrid cloud solutions provide the agility of the public cloud when needed, while also allowing you to maintain control over your sensitive data on the private cloud. This flexibility is like having the ability to adjust your menu based on special occasions or seasonal ingredients, while still offering core customer favorites.

Cost Optimization: By strategically allocating workloads, you can leverage the cost-effectiveness of the public cloud for specific tasks, while keeping critical operations within the controlled environment of your private cloud. It's like optimizing your menu to offer budget-friendly options alongside premium dishes, catering to a wider range of customers without sacrificing profitability.

Key Considerations for Hybrid Cloud:

Network Connectivity: Ensuring seamless and secure data flow between your private and public cloud environments is crucial. It's like having a well-coordinated wait staff who can efficiently deliver orders between the kitchen (private cloud) and the dining area (public cloud).

Management Complexity: Managing a hybrid cloud requires careful planning and coordination. Standardized processes and tools are essential for smooth operation. Think of it as having well-defined protocols for communication and collaboration between your chefs and the staff managing your external supplier deliveries.

Security Measures: Robust security protocols are essential to protect your data across both environments.

Just like a restaurant prioritizes food safety, you need strong security measures to ensure the integrity of your data in both the private and public cloud.

Benefits of Hybrid Cloud Solutions:

- **Enhanced Agility and Scalability:** Respond to changing business needs by seamlessly scaling resources in the public cloud while maintaining control over core applications in the private cloud. This adaptability allows you to cater to fluctuating customer demands, just like a restaurant can adjust its menu based on peak seasons or special events.

- **Improved Disaster Recovery:** A private cloud environment acts as a backup in case of outages in the public cloud. This redundancy ensures business continuity, similar to having a backup kitchen prepared in case of unexpected issues with your main kitchen.

- **Optimized Costs:** Pay only for the public cloud resources you use, while keeping control of sensitive data within your private cloud. This cost-effective approach is like having a menu that offers both high-end ingredients and budget-friendly options, appealing to a broader range of customers without compromising on quality.

Hybrid cloud solutions offer a versatile approach to cloud computing. By carefully considering your business needs and adopting the right mix of public and private cloud resources, you can create a digital menu that delivers optimal performance, security, and cost-effectiveness for your organization. This allows you to focus on your core business objectives, just like a restaurant owner can focus on delivering exceptional customer experiences with the right combination of in-house and outsourced resources.

CHAPTER FOUR

CLOUD ARCHITECTURE

The "essential equipment" in cloud infrastructure translates to core services like compute resources (virtual machines), storage (for data), and networking (for communication). These are the foundational elements for any cloud deployment.

Specialized Tools:

Kitchen: Specialized tools like a pizza oven or a deep fryer cater to specific culinary styles. They improve efficiency for particular tasks.

Cloud Infrastructure: Cloud platforms offer a wide range of specialized services beyond the core options. These include databases, analytics tools, machine learning platforms, and containerization services. They cater to specific needs and workloads.

Menu vs. Business Needs:

Kitchen: The type of cuisine you cook dictates your equipment choices. A pizzeria needs a powerful oven, while a bakery might prioritize a proofing cabinet.

Cloud Infrastructure: Your business needs determine the cloud infrastructure you choose. A data analytics company requires robust storage and processing power, while an e-commerce platform prioritizes scalability and security.

Choosing the Right Equipment for the Job:

Kitchen: Choosing the right size and capacity for your equipment is crucial. An oversized oven for a small kitchen is wasteful, while an underpowered one hinders productivity.

Cloud Infrastructure: Similar to kitchen equipment, cloud resources come in various sizes and configurations. Analyze your workload and choose resources (virtual machines) with the right processing power and memory to handle your needs efficiently, avoiding overspending.

Scalability:

Kitchen: A growing restaurant might need to upgrade its equipment to handle increased demand.

Cloud Infrastructure: The beauty of cloud infrastructure is its inherent scalability. You can easily add or remove resources like virtual machines and storage as your business needs fluctuate.

The "kitchen equipment" analogy for selecting cloud infrastructure:

1. **Identify your business needs:** Analyze your applications' resource requirements (processing power, storage) and workload patterns.
2. **Choose the core services:** Select the essential cloud infrastructure components – compute, storage, and networking – based on your size and needs.
3. **Explore specialized services:** Investigate the cloud platform's additional services like databases or analytics tools that can enhance your operations.
4. **Right-size your resources:** Don't overprovision. Choose resources with the right capacity to avoid unnecessary

costs.

5. **Plan for scaling:** Select a cloud platform that allows for easy scaling of resources as your business grows.

By carefully considering your business needs and adopting this "kitchen equipment" approach, you can select the most suitable cloud infrastructure for your operations, ensuring efficient performance and cost-effectiveness.

KITCHEN STAFF : MANAGING CLOUD RESOURCES

The skilled staff in a kitchen keeps everything running smoothly. Similarly, effective cloud resource management requires the right approach and expertise. Here's how the kitchen staff analogy translates to managing cloud resources:

Team Roles:

Kitchen Staff: A well-functioning kitchen has a team with specialized roles – head chef (overseeing operations), line cooks (executing tasks), and prep cooks (preparing ingredients).

Cloud Resource Management: Cloud resource management also benefits from a designated team. This team can include a cloud architect (designing the infrastructure), cloud engineers (provisioning and managing resources), and cloud cost analysts (optimizing spending).

Following Recipes (Instructions):

Kitchen Staff: Cooks follow recipes to ensure consistent quality and efficient preparation.

Cloud Resource Management: Cloud resources are provisioned and managed based on pre-defined configurations, like "recipes," to ensure consistent performance and avoid errors. Infrastructure as code (IaC) tools automate these configurations, acting like the recipes for cloud resources.

Monitoring and Adapting:

Kitchen Staff: Experienced chefs monitor cooking processes and adjust parameters (heat, timing) as needed to ensure optimal results.

Cloud Resource Management: Cloud monitoring tools track resource usage and performance. Just like chefs adapt their cooking, cloud managers can scale resources up or down (add or remove virtual machines) based on real-time demands, optimizing performance and cost.

Cleanliness and Efficiency:

Kitchen Staff: Maintaining a clean and organized kitchen is crucial for efficiency and hygiene.

Cloud Resource Management: Regularly cleaning up unused resources (idle virtual machines, redundant storage) in the cloud ensures optimal resource utilization and avoids unnecessary costs. This is akin to keeping your kitchen organized and avoiding clutter.

Communication and Collaboration:

Kitchen Staff: Effective communication between chefs, cooks, and other staff is essential for smooth kitchen operations.

Cloud Resource Management: Collaboration between cloud management teams, developers, and other stakeholders ensures resources are aligned with business needs.

The "kitchen staff" analogy for managing cloud resources:

1. **Build a cloud management team:** Establish a team with the right skills to handle cloud architecture, resource provisioning, and cost optimization.

2. **Define infrastructure as code (IaC):** Create standardized configurations for provisioning and managing cloud resources, ensuring consistency and repeatability.

3. **Implement cloud monitoring tools:** Proactively monitor resource usage and performance to identify areas for optimization.

4. **Practice regular resource hygiene:** Clean up unused resources to streamline your cloud environment and avoid unnecessary spending.

5. **Foster communication and collaboration:** Ensure clear communication between cloud management, developers, and other stakeholders to align resources with business goals.

By adopting this "kitchen staff" approach, you can establish a well-oiled cloud resource management strategy that ensures efficiency, performance, and cost-effectiveness for your cloud infrastructure.

CHAPTER FIVE

MENU TESTING : CLOUD PILOT PROJECTS

A restaurant wouldn't launch a full menu without testing, businesses shouldn't jump into a complex cloud environment headfirst. Here's how the concept of "menu testing" translates to cloud pilot projects:

Refining the Menu:

Restaurant: Before unveiling a new menu, restaurants might test dishes with a limited audience to receive feedback and refine recipes. This ensures the final menu offers delicious and well-received options.

Cloud Pilot Projects: Cloud pilot projects act as a testing ground for your cloud strategy. By deploying a small-scale version of your intended cloud environment, you can identify potential issues, optimize configurations, and ensure your chosen services meet your needs before fully committing.

Identifying the Right Fit:

Restaurant: Menu testing helps identify dishes that don't travel well or take too long to prepare, ensuring a smooth dining experience.

Cloud Pilot Projects: Cloud pilot projects allow you to assess the performance of specific cloud services and configurations. You can test scalability, security measures, and integration with existing systems before a full-scale deployment.

Cost-Effective Experimentation:

Restaurant: Testing dishes on a small scale allows for cost-effective experimentation with new recipes before committing to a full menu rollout.

Cloud Pilot Projects: Cloud pilot projects are a cost-effective way to experiment with different cloud solutions and configurations. You only pay for the limited resources used during the testing phase, minimizing financial risk.

Gathering Feedback and Iteration:

Restaurant: Feedback from menu testing helps refine recipes and presentation based on customer preferences. This ensures the final menu resonates with the target audience.

Cloud Pilot Projects: Cloud pilot projects provide valuable insights into performance, scalability, and overall effectiveness. Based on this feedback, you can iterate on your cloud strategy and configurations for optimal results.

Benefits of Cloud Pilot Projects:

By adopting the "menu testing" approach with cloud pilot projects, you gain several benefits:

1. **Reduced Risk:** Identify and address potential issues before a full-scale cloud deployment.
2. **Improved Performance:** Optimize configurations for efficient resource utilization and application performance.

3. **Cost Savings:** Avoid costly mistakes by testing different cloud solutions before committing to one.
4. **Enhanced Security:** Test security measures in a controlled environment to ensure a secure cloud environment.
5. **Informed Decision Making:** Gather data and gain insights to make informed choices about your cloud strategy.

Cloud pilot projects, just like menu testing for restaurants, are a crucial step in ensuring a successful cloud migration or deployment. By taking the time to test and refine your cloud strategy through pilot projects, you can avoid costly mistakes and lay the groundwork for a high-performing, secure, and cost-effective cloud environment.

MENU OPTIMIZATION : CONTINUOUS CLOUD IMPROVEMENT

A successful restaurant constantly tweaks its menu to stay ahead of the curve, continuous improvement is the key ingredient for a thriving cloud environment. Here's how the concept of "menu optimization" translates to the world of cloud computing:

Keeping Your Menu Fresh:

Restaurant: A thriving restaurant doesn't simply launch a static menu. They analyze customer preferences, food trends, and seasonal ingredients to keep their offerings exciting and relevant. This ensures a steady stream of satisfied diners.

Cloud Optimization: Cloud environments require constant monitoring and fine-tuning to guarantee they remain efficient, cost-effective, and aligned with your evolving business needs. Just like a menu refresh, cloud optimization keeps your virtual infrastructure dynamic and responsive to changing demands.

Analyzing Customer Preferences:

Restaurant: Restaurants leverage sales data and customer feedback to identify popular dishes and areas for improvement. This allows them to tailor their menu to better serve their clientele.

Cloud Optimization: Cloud monitoring tools provide valuable insights into resource usage, application performance, and potential bottlenecks. This data acts as your "customer feedback" in the cloud, helping you identify areas for optimization, such as scaling resources or adjusting configurations to ensure peak performance.

Seasonal Tweaks:

Restaurant: Menus often change seasonally to incorporate fresh, local ingredients and cater to changing customer preferences throughout the year. A summer menu might feature lighter options, while winter offerings might focus on comfort food.

Cloud Optimization: Your cloud environment might also require adjustments based on seasonal workload fluctuations. For example, e-commerce platforms might need to scale up resources during peak shopping seasons to handle increased traffic. By optimizing your cloud infrastructure for these predictable fluctuations, you ensure smooth operations and a positive customer experience.

Cost Control and Efficiency:

Restaurant: Restaurants regularly review their menus to identify high-cost ingredients or dishes with low profit margins. They might adjust recipes or remove underperforming items to optimize profitability.

Cloud Optimization: Regularly analyzing cloud costs helps identify potential areas for savings. You can explore options like reserved instances or spot pricing for unused resources, similar to a restaurant optimizing its menu for profitability. This ensures you're not paying for virtual "ingredients" you don't need.

The Continuous Improvement Cycle:

Restaurant: Successful restaurants have a feedback loop – analyze customer data, refine the menu, gather more feedback, and iterate again. This cycle ensures continuous improvement and customer satisfaction.

Cloud Optimization: Cloud optimization follows a similar cycle. Monitor performance, identify areas for improvement, implement changes based on the data, and continue monitoring to maintain ongoing effectiveness. This iterative approach ensures your cloud environment stays perfectly calibrated to your business needs.

Benefits of Continuous Cloud Optimization:

By adopting a "menu optimization" approach to cloud improvement, you gain several advantages:

1. **Reduced Costs:** Identify and eliminate wasteful spending on underutilized resources.
2. **Improved Performance:** Optimize configurations for efficient resource utilization and application performance.
3. **Enhanced Security:** Continuously monitor and update security measures to address evolving threats.
4. **Increased Scalability:** Ensure your cloud environment can adapt to changing workloads and future growth.
5. **Dynamic Cloud Environment:** Maintain a cloud environment that is agile and responsive to your evolving business needs.

Remember, cloud environments are dynamic, not static. By following a "menu optimization" approach and continuously monitoring, analyzing, and refining your cloud strategy, you can ensure your virtual kitchen remains efficient, cost-effective, and perfectly suited to meet the ever-changing demands of your business. This continuous improvement ensures your cloud infrastructure serves as the foundation for success, just like a well-crafted menu fuels a thriving restaurant

CHAPTER SIX

CLOUD DINNING EXPERIENCE

Cloud dining, a relatively new concept, offers a unique and exciting way to experience fine dining. Imagine a luxurious meal suspended high above the city skyline, breathtaking views as your backdrop. Cloud dining restaurants utilize cranes to hoist specially designed platforms, transforming them into temporary fine-dining havens. While enjoying meticulously prepared courses, guests can marvel at the panoramic vistas, creating an unforgettable and truly extraordinary dining experience. However, this exclusivity comes at a price, as cloud dining is typically a premium offering.

CUSTOMER SATISFACTION : MONITORING CLOUD PERFORMANCE

In today's digital world, customer satisfaction hinges on a seamless and efficient online experience. This is especially true for businesses that rely on cloud-based platforms to deliver their services. Just like a smooth-running kitchen ensures happy diners in a restaurant, monitoring cloud performance is crucial for keeping your customers satisfied. Here's why:

Performance Impacts Perception:

Slow Service: Imagine a restaurant where service is slow, and food arrives cold. Customers are likely to be frustrated and leave with a negative impression.

Cloud Performance: Similarly, slow loading times, application unavailability, or frequent outages in your cloud-based service can lead to customer frustration and churn.

Monitoring for a Positive Experience:

Attentive Staff: A good restaurant has attentive staff who anticipate customer needs and address any issues promptly.

Cloud Monitoring: Proactive cloud performance monitoring acts like your attentive staff in the digital world. It identifies potential issues before they impact customers, allowing you to take corrective action and ensure a smooth user experience.

Identifying Bottlenecks:

Kitchen Backlog: A restaurant might monitor kitchen wait times to identify bottlenecks in food preparation, allowing them to optimize their processes.

Cloud Monitoring: Cloud monitoring tools pinpoint performance bottlenecks within your cloud environment. Is it slow database queries, insufficient server resources, or network congestion? Identifying these bottlenecks allows you to optimize your cloud infrastructure for better performance.

Maintaining Uptime and Availability:

Restaurant Closures: A restaurant closure due to unforeseen circumstances disrupts customer plans and creates frustration.

Cloud Downtime: Cloud outages or downtime can have a similar disruptive effect on your customers who rely on your service. Monitoring ensures you're alerted to potential issues and can take steps to minimize downtime.

Building Trust and Confidence:

Consistent Quality: Customers appreciate a restaurant that consistently delivers delicious food and excellent service.

Reliable Cloud Performance: By consistently monitoring and optimizing your cloud performance, you ensure your service is reliable and available for your customers, fostering trust and confidence.

Leverage cloud performance monitoring for customer satisfaction:

1. **Implement cloud monitoring tools:** Track key metrics like uptime, response times, and resource utilization.
2. **Set performance thresholds:** Define acceptable performance levels and receive alerts when metrics fall outside these ranges.
3. **Analyze data and identify bottlenecks:** Investigate the root cause of performance issues and take corrective action.
4. **Proactive maintenance:** Regularly update software and perform routine maintenance to prevent problems.

By prioritizing cloud performance monitoring, you can ensure your customers experience a smooth, reliable, and efficient service. This, in turn, translates to higher customer satisfaction, loyalty, and ultimately, business success. Remember, happy customers are the foundation of any thriving business, and in the digital world, cloud performance plays a critical role in achieving that happiness.

GUEST FEEDBACK : CLOUD ANALYTICS AND OPTIMIZATION

In the world of hospitality, guest feedback is a goldmine of information. It allows hotels and restaurants to understand their strengths and weaknesses, identify areas for improvement, and ultimately, enhance the guest experience. Just like analyzing guest feedback is crucial for a successful restaurant, cloud analytics play a vital role in optimizing your cloud environment. Here's how the analogy translates:

Understanding Guest Preferences:

Guest Feedback: Restaurants analyze feedback to understand guest preferences regarding food, service, and ambiance. This helps them tailor their offerings to better serve their clientele.

Cloud Analytics: Cloud analytics tools provide insights into resource usage, application performance, and user behavior within your cloud environment. This data helps you understand how your cloud infrastructure is being used and identify areas for optimization.

Identifying Service Issues:

Guest Feedback: Negative feedback about slow service or long wait times might indicate operational inefficiencies in the kitchen or inadequate staffing.

Cloud Analytics: Performance bottlenecks within your cloud environment can manifest as slow loading times, application crashes, or frequent outages. Cloud analytics helps identify these issues before they significantly impact your users.

Prioritizing Guest Concerns:

Guest Feedback: Restaurants might prioritize addressing frequent complaints about specific dishes or service aspects based on the volume and nature of guest feedback.

Cloud Analytics: Cloud analytics helps you prioritize optimization efforts by highlighting critical issues with the greatest impact on user experience. Are slow database queries causing delays, or is insufficient server capacity leading to outages? Focusing on the most impactful areas ensures efficient optimization.

Data-Driven Decision Making:

Guest Feedback: Relying solely on intuition for menu changes or service adjustments can be risky. Restaurants leverage guest feedback data to make informed decisions about their operations.

Cloud Analytics: Data-driven decision making is crucial for cloud optimization. Cloud analytics provide the insights needed to understand resource allocation, identify scaling needs, and choose the most suitable cloud services for your specific requirements.

Optimizing for a Better Experience:

Guest Feedback: Positive guest feedback motivates restaurants to maintain their high standards and continuously improve their offerings.

Cloud Analytics: By optimizing your cloud environment based on data-driven insights from analytics, you can ensure a smooth, reliable, and efficient experience for your users. This translates to a positive "cloud experience" for your customers or business partners who rely on your cloud-based services.

Guest feedback and cloud analytics for optimization:

1. **Collect and analyze user feedback:** Gather feedback through surveys, support tickets, and social media monitoring.
2. **Utilize cloud analytics tools:** Implement tools to track resource usage, application performance, and user

behavior within your cloud environment.

3. **Combine data analysis with feedback:** Correlate guest feedback with cloud analytics insights to identify areas needing improvement.
4. **Prioritize optimization efforts:** Focus on addressing the most critical issues identified through combined data analysis and guest feedback.
5. **Measure and iterate:** Track the impact of optimization efforts on cloud performance and user experience, and continuously refine your strategy based on the results.

By following these steps, you can transform guest feedback and cloud analytics into a powerful force for optimizing your cloud environment. This, in turn, translates to a more efficient, reliable, and user-friendly experience for everyone who interacts with your cloud services. Remember, just like happy guests are the lifeblood of a successful restaurant, a well-optimized cloud environment is the foundation for delivering exceptional experiences in the digital world.

REPEAT BUSINESS : CLOUD COST MANAGEMENT

In the world of restaurants, repeat business is crucial for success. Customers who have a positive dining experience are more likely to return and recommend your establishment to others. Similarly, in the world of cloud computing, cost management is essential for ensuring long-term sustainability and fostering repeat business with your cloud provider. Here's how the concept of "repeat business" translates to cloud cost management:

Building Trust and Value:

Restaurant: A restaurant that consistently delivers delicious food and excellent service at a fair price builds trust and loyalty with its customers, leading to repeat visits.

Cloud Cost Management: By effectively managing your cloud costs, you optimize your spending and ensure you're getting the most value from your cloud provider. This builds trust and encourages long-term partnerships.

Understanding Customer Needs:

Restaurant: A successful restaurant understands its customers' needs and preferences. They might offer loyalty programs or cater to specific dietary restrictions to keep customers coming back.

Cloud Cost Management: Understanding your cloud usage patterns and resource needs allows you to choose the most cost-effective pricing models and services offered by your cloud provider. This ensures you're not paying for unnecessary features.

Avoiding Surprises:

Restaurant: A restaurant with fluctuating prices or surprise menu changes might deter customers from returning. Predictability fosters trust.

Cloud Cost Management: Unforeseen cloud costs can be a major shock. Cloud cost management practices like cost forecasting and reserved instances help avoid unexpected bills and ensure budget predictability.

Optimizing for Long-Term Value:

Restaurant: Restaurants might offer special deals or promotions to incentivize repeat business and encourage customers to explore new menu items.

Cloud Cost Management: Optimizing your cloud environment for long-term value involves rightsizing resources, leveraging spot instances, and negotiating committed use discounts with your cloud provider. These measures maximize your return on investment (ROI) from the cloud.

Benefits of Effective Cloud Cost Management:

By adopting a "repeat business" approach to cloud cost management, you gain several advantages:

1. **Reduced Costs:** Eliminate wasteful spending on unused or underutilized cloud resources.
2. **Improved Profitability:** Optimize your cloud budget for long-term financial sustainability.
3. **Enhanced Cloud Security:** Cost management practices can help identify and eliminate potential security risks associated with unused resources.
4. **Stronger Vendor Relationships:** Effective cost management fosters trust and can lead to better pricing negotiations with your cloud provider.
5. **Informed Cloud Decisions:** Cost data insights help you make informed decisions about resource allocation and future cloud investments.

Building a Sustainable Cloud Strategy:

Just like a restaurant owner wouldn't simply open their doors and wait for customers, effective cloud cost management requires a proactive approach. Here are some key practices:

- **Monitor and Analyze Cloud Costs:** Track your cloud spending and identify areas for optimization.
- **Implement Cost Allocation Strategies:** Allocate cloud costs accurately to different departments or projects within your organization.
- **Rightsize Your Cloud Resources:** Ensure you're using the appropriate amount of resources for your needs.
- **Utilize Reserved Instances and Spot Instances:** Leverage these pricing models to optimize your cloud spend for predictable and variable workloads.

- **Negotiate with Your Cloud Provider:** Consider negotiating committed use discounts or custom pricing plans based on your specific usage patterns.

By prioritizing cloud cost management, you cultivate a "repeat business" mindset with your cloud provider. This ensures you get the most value out of your cloud investment, fosters long-term sustainability, and positions your organization for success in the ever-evolving world of cloud computing. Remember, a well-managed cloud environment, just like a well-run restaurant, attracts and retains customers (or in this case, cloud users) through a combination of value, efficiency, and a commitment to long-term satisfaction.

CHAPTER SEVEN

CLOUD SECURITY

Digital age, businesses are increasingly migrating their operations to the cloud. This shift offers numerous advantages, including scalability, agility, and cost-effectiveness. However, with this transition comes a critical responsibility – ensuring the security of your valuable data and applications residing in the cloud. Cloud security encompasses a comprehensive set of policies, technologies, and controls designed to safeguard your digital assets in this virtual environment.Unlike traditional on-premise IT infrastructure, where you have complete physical control over your servers and data, cloud security involves a shared responsibility model. Cloud providers are responsible for securing the underlying infrastructure, while businesses are entrusted with securing their data, applications, and access controls within the cloud environment. This necessitates a proactive approach to cloud security, requiring organizations to understand the potential threats, implement robust security measures, and continuously monitor and adapt their strategies.

The cloud security landscape is constantly evolving, with new threats emerging alongside advancements in cloud technologies. Malicious actors are continuously devising sophisticated techniques to exploit vulnerabilities and gain unauthorized access to sensitive data.

FOOD SAFETY : CLOUD SECURITY BEST PRATICES

Food safety is paramount for a successful restaurant, prioritizing cloud security is essential for any business leveraging the cloud. Here's how the analogy of food safety translates to best practices for cloud security:

Fresh Ingredients: Data Security

Restaurant: Fresh, high-quality ingredients are crucial for delicious and safe meals.

Cloud Security: Implementing robust data encryption safeguards your sensitive information in the cloud, similar to storing food in airtight containers to prevent spoilage. Encryption acts as a digital barrier, protecting your data from unauthorized access.

Proper Storage: Access Controls

Restaurant: Food items are stored appropriately to prevent contamination and maintain freshness.

Cloud Security: Enforcing strict access controls ensures only authorized users can access specific data within your cloud environment. This is like following designated storage areas for different food items in a restaurant – raw meat wouldn't be stored next to vegetables to prevent cross-contamination.

Temperature Control: Monitoring and Logging

Restaurant: Maintaining proper temperatures during food storage and preparation is vital to prevent bacterial growth.

Cloud Security: Continuously monitoring your cloud environment for suspicious activity and maintaining detailed logs is crucial for identifying and responding to potential security breaches. This is like regularly checking food temperatures with thermometers and keeping detailed records to ensure everything stays within safe zones.

Cleanliness and Hygiene: Patch Management

Restaurant: Maintaining a clean kitchen and following proper hygiene practices is essential to prevent foodborne illnesses.

Cloud Security: Regularly patching and updating software within your cloud environment ensures you have the latest security fixes and minimizes vulnerabilities that could be exploited by attackers. This is like keeping your kitchen equipment clean and sanitized to prevent the spread of germs.

Pest Control: Threat Detection

Restaurant: Implementing measures to control pests like rodents and insects protects food from contamination.

Cloud Security: Utilizing threat detection tools helps identify and mitigate potential security threats before they can compromise your cloud environment. Imagine these tools as digital pest traps, constantly monitoring for and eliminating potential security risks.

Staff Training: Security Awareness

Restaurant: Training staff on food safety protocols ensures they handle food properly and maintain hygiene standards.

Cloud Security: Providing security awareness training to your employees empowers them to identify and avoid potential security risks. This is like training your restaurant staff on proper food handling procedures to prevent contamination.

Regular Inspections: Penetration Testing

Restaurant: Regular health inspections ensure restaurants adhere to food safety regulations.

Cloud Security: Conducting penetration testing simulates real-world attacks, helping identify weaknesses in your cloud security posture. Penetration testing acts like a mock health inspection, proactively uncovering any areas where your security measures might need improvement.

The Benefits of Cloud Security Best Practices

By adopting these "food safety" best practices for cloud security, you gain several advantages:

1. **Data Protection:** Safeguard your sensitive information from unauthorized access and data breaches.
2. **Enhanced Compliance:** Meet industry regulations and data privacy requirements.
3. **Business Continuity:** Minimize disruptions and ensure the availability of your cloud-based applications and data.
4. **Reduced Risk:** Proactively address vulnerabilities and prevent costly security incidents.
5. **Customer Trust:** Foster trust with your customers and partners by demonstrating your commitment to data security.

Cloud security is not a one-time fix; it's an ongoing process. By prioritizing these "food safety" best practices, you can cultivate a culture of security within your organization and ensure your cloud environment is well-protected. Remember, just like a clean and well-maintained kitchen is the foundation for a successful restaurant, robust cloud security is essential for a thriving digital business in today's cloud-driven world.

PROTECTION FROM THIEVES : IDENTITY AND ACCESS MANAHEMENT

Imagine your identity as your house, filled with valuables you want to protect. Identity and Access Management (IAM) is like a high-tech security system for your digital home. It ensures only authorized individuals (guests) can enter specific areas (access resources) and prevents unwanted visitors (unauthorized users) from gaining access to your valuables (sensitive data).

The Problem:

In today's digital world, our identities are spread across numerous online accounts and services. This creates a vast attack surface for cybercriminals, who act like digital thieves trying to break into our digital homes to steal valuable information like financial data, personal details, or intellectual property.

IAM: Your Digital Security System

IAM offers a multi-layered approach to securing your digital identity and data. Here's how it works:

Identification: IAM verifies the identity of anyone trying to access your digital resources. This is like having a secure entry system that checks a visitor's ID before allowing them in.

Authentication: Once identity is confirmed, IAM requires users to prove they are who they claim to be. This is like having multiple layers of authentication, such as a password and a fingerprint scan, to ensure only the authorized person enters.

Authorization: Even after successful authentication, IAM determines what level of access a user has. Imagine assigning different access levels to guests – a close friend might have access to the living room, while a delivery person might only have access to the doorstep.

Benefits of Strong IAM:

- Reduced Risk of Data Breaches: IAM makes it significantly harder for unauthorized users to gain access to sensitive information.

- Enhanced Compliance: Many regulations require organizations to have robust IAM practices in place.
- Improved Productivity: Streamlined access management saves time and frustration for authorized users.
- Reduced Costs: Strong IAM can help prevent costly data breaches and security incidents.

Key IAM Practices:

- **Strong Passwords and Multi-Factor Authentication (MFA):** Enforce the use of complex passwords and implement MFA, which requires additional verification factors beyond just a password. Imagine using a strong lock on your door and also having a security guard verify a guest's identity before letting them in.
- **Least Privilege Access:** Grant users the minimum level of access required to perform their jobs. This principle ensures that even if a thief gains entry (unauthorized access), they can only access a limited amount of valuables (data).
- **Regular User Access Reviews:** Periodically review user access privileges to ensure they remain appropriate. Think of this as regularly reviewing and updating the guest list for your digital home.

In today's digital landscape, IAM is no longer an option; it's a necessity. By implementing robust IAM practices, you can significantly reduce the risk of identity theft, data breaches, and other security threats. Remember, your digital identity and data are valuable assets. Just like you wouldn't leave your house unlocked and unguarded, prioritize IAM to safeguard your digital home and keep your valuables safe.

DATA BACKUP AND RECOVERY

Imagine your life's most precious photos and documents stored on a single computer. Data backup and recovery is like having a secure vault for your irreplaceable digital memories, ensuring you don't lose them due to unforeseen events.

Data Backup and Recovery Important

Data loss can occur due to various reasons:

- **Hardware Failure:** Physical damage to storage devices like hard drives can lead to data loss.
- **Software Corruption:** Software malfunctions or attacks by viruses and malware can corrupt your data.
- **Accidental Deletion:** Human error, such as accidentally deleting important files, can be a major cause of data loss.
- **Natural Disasters:** Floods, fires, or other natural disasters can damage your physical storage devices and the data they contain.

Data backup and recovery offers a critical safety net by creating copies of your data and storing them in a separate location. This allows you to restore your data in case of any unforeseen events.

The Backup and Recovery Process:

1. **Data Selection:** Identify the critical data you need to back up, such as documents, photos, emails, and financial records.
2. **Backup Frequency:** Determine how often you need to back up your data, depending on how frequently it changes.

3. **Backup Destination:** Choose a secure and reliable location to store your backups, such as an external hard drive, a cloud storage service, or a combination of both.
4. **Recovery Process:** Establish a clear procedure for restoring your data in case of an emergency.

Types of Data Backups:

- **Full Backups:** Create a complete copy of all your data at a specific point in time.
- **Incremental Backups:** Only back up files that have changed since the last backup.
- **Differential Backups:** Back up all files that have changed since the last full backup.

Benefits of Data Backup and Recovery:

- **Peace of Mind:** Knowing your data is safeguarded provides peace of mind and reduces stress.
- **Disaster Recovery:** Enables quick recovery from data loss events, minimizing downtime and ensuring business continuity.
- **Improved Security:** Backups offer an extra layer of protection against ransomware attacks, as you can restore your data without paying the attacker's demands.
- **Compliance:** Some industries have regulations requiring organizations to maintain backups of their data.

Data Backup and Recovery Best Practices:

Follow the 3-2-1 rule: Maintain at least 3 copies of your data, on 2 different storage media, with 1 copy stored offsite.

Test your backups regularly: Ensure your backups are functional and can be restored successfully.

Secure your backups: Encrypt your backups to add an extra layer of protection.

Data backup and recovery is an essential practice for anyone who values their digital information. By implementing a robust backup and recovery strategy, you can safeguard your precious memories and ensure your business or personal data is always protected. Remember, data loss can be devastating, but with a well-planned backup and recovery solution, you can prevent disaster and ensure your digital life remains secure

CHAPTER EIGHT

CLOUD SCALING

Cloud scaling is a fundamental concept in cloud computing that empowers businesses to dynamically adjust their resource allocation based on changing demands. Unlike traditional on-premise IT infrastructure, where resources are static and often underutilized or overloaded, the cloud offers elasticity. This elasticity allows you to scale your resources up or down, similar to how you might adjust the size of your team or equipment depending on project requirements. There are two main types of cloud scaling: vertical scaling (also known as scaling up or down) and horizontal scaling (also known as scaling in or out). Vertical scaling involves modifying the processing power, memory, or storage capacity of an existing cloud server. Imagine adding more cores to a CPU or increasing the RAM on your computer for improved performance. Horizontal scaling, on the other hand, involves adding or removing entire servers from your cloud environment. This is like bringing on additional team members or renting more office space to accommodate a growing workload. By effectively utilizing cloud scaling, businesses can achieve several advantages. They can optimize costs by paying only for the resources they use, ensure application performance and availability during traffic spikes, and foster agility to adapt to evolving business needs. Cloud scaling is a game-changer for businesses of all sizes, enabling them to leverage the power of the cloud without being confined by the limitations of fixed infrastructure.

SCALING CLOUD RESOURCES

Imagine your business blossoming – new customers, increased sales, and exciting opportunities on the horizon. But can your current infrastructure keep up? This is where cloud scaling comes in, acting as the fertilizer that helps your business flourish in the digital landscape. Just like you wouldn't plant a sprawling garden in a tiny pot, cloud scaling allows you to dynamically adjust your cloud resources to accommodate your growing business needs.

Why Scale in the Cloud?

Cost-Effectiveness: Pay only for the resources you use. With cloud scaling, you're not stuck with underutilized hardware or struggling with overloaded servers. You can scale up during peak demand periods and scale down during slower times, optimizing your spending.

Improved Performance: Ensure a smooth user experience for your customers. By scaling resources up when needed, you can prevent application slowdowns or crashes during traffic spikes. Imagine having enough staff on hand to handle a busy sales day – cloud scaling ensures your resources can handle increased customer demand.

Enhanced Agility: Adapt quickly to changing market conditions. Cloud scaling allows you to easily add new resources or adjust existing ones as your business evolves. This agility is like having a team that can quickly pivot and take on new projects as opportunities arise.

Scalability on Demand: No upfront investment in hardware. The cloud eliminates the need for expensive upfront investments in hardware that might become obsolete quickly. Cloud scaling allows you to access resources as needed, eliminating the risk of over- or under-provisioning.

Scaling Strategies for Growth:

Vertical Scaling (Scale Up): Increase the processing power, memory, or storage capacity of your existing cloud servers. Think of it as giving your star performers in the IT department more powerful tools to work with.

Horizontal Scaling (Scale Out): Add more virtual servers to your cloud environment to distribute the workload. Imagine expanding your team by bringing in additional experts to handle specific tasks.

Auto Scaling: Leverage automation tools that automatically adjust resources based on predefined triggers, such as CPU usage or number of active users. This is like having a smart irrigation system that waters your plants based on real-time sensor data.

Scaling for Success: A Proactive Approach

Monitor and Analyze Usage: Keep track of your cloud resource consumption to identify usage patterns and potential bottlenecks. Regular checkups are crucial for any growing business!

Plan for Future Growth: Anticipate future business needs and proactively scale your resources to avoid disruptions during growth spurts. Think of it as having a business plan that outlines future staffing and resource requirements.

Choose the Right Cloud Provider: Select a cloud provider that offers flexible scaling options and a variety of resource types to cater to your specific needs. Just like choosing the right soil and fertilizer for your plants, pick a cloud provider that offers the most suitable resources for your business growth.

Cloud scaling empowers businesses to break free from the constraints of fixed infrastructure. By adopting a proactive approach to cloud scaling, you can ensure your digital environment grows and adapts alongside your business. Remember, successful businesses are constantly evolving. Cloud scaling provides the flexibility and agility to ensure your digital foundation keeps pace with your ambitions, allowing you to focus on nurturing your business and cultivating success.

AUTO SCALING

Online store automatically hiring more staff (adding resources) during peak holiday sales and reducing staff during slower periods. That's the magic of auto scaling in cloud computing – it takes the manual effort out of resource allocation, allowing your cloud environment to adjust on its own, just like a self-driving car navigating traffic.

Why Use Auto Scaling?

Effortless Efficiency: Auto scaling automates the process of scaling cloud resources up or down based on predefined metrics. This frees you from constantly monitoring and manually adjusting resources, allowing you to focus on other strategic tasks.

Cost Optimization: By automatically scaling down during low-demand periods, you avoid paying for unused resources. Conversely, auto scaling ensures you have enough resources to handle surges in traffic, preventing performance issues and potential revenue loss.

Improved Application Performance: Auto scaling prevents application slowdowns or crashes by automatically adding resources when demand increases. This translates to a smooth and seamless user experience for your customers, just like having enough staff on hand to ensure efficient service during busy periods.

Enhanced Scalability: Auto scaling allows your cloud environment to adapt to unpredictable traffic patterns. Whether you experience sudden spikes or gradual growth, auto scaling ensures you have the resources needed to maintain optimal performance.

Auto Scaling Work

1. **Define Scaling Policies:** You set the rules for auto scaling by specifying metrics like CPU usage, memory consumption, or number of active users. These metrics act as the road signs for your auto scaling car.
2. **Monitoring and Triggers:** The cloud platform continuously monitors your chosen metrics. When a predefined threshold is reached (like a traffic jam ahead), auto scaling is triggered.
3. **Automatic Scaling Actions:** Based on the policy you defined (adding or removing resources), the cloud platform automatically scales your resources up or down. This is like your auto scaling car adding more lanes to the highway during congestion or switching to a smaller route during lighter traffic.

Benefits of Auto Scaling:

- **Reduced Management Overhead:** Automates resource allocation, freeing up your IT team to focus on other priorities.
- **Improved Cost Control:** Pays only for the resources you use, optimizing your cloud spending.
- **Enhanced Application Availability:** Ensures applications remain responsive and available even during traffic spikes.

- **Increased Business Agility:** Allows your cloud environment to seamlessly adapt to changing business needs.

Auto Scaling Best Practices:

- **Start Simple:** Begin with basic auto scaling policies based on a single metric. As you gain experience, you can create more complex policies with multiple triggers.
- **Thorough Testing:** Test your auto scaling policies in a non-production environment before deploying them to ensure they function as expected.
- **Monitor and Refine:** Continuously monitor your auto scaling performance and adjust policies as needed to optimize resource usage and application performance.

Auto scaling is a powerful tool that can transform your cloud experience. By automating resource allocation, you gain efficiency, cost savings, and improved application performance. Just like autopilot allows you to focus on enjoying the journey in a self-driving car, auto scaling empowers you to focus on growing your business while your cloud environment seamlessly scales to meet your needs.

AVOIDING OVERSTOCKING : CLOUD COST OPTIMIZATION

Warehouse is overflowing with unsold inventory (unused resources) eating into your profits. Cloud cost optimization is like the savvy inventory management system for your digital warehouse (cloud environment). It helps you avoid overstocking on cloud resources, ensuring you pay only for what you actually use.

Cloud Cost Optimization Important

Hidden Costs: Cloud services can be deceptively inexpensive at first glance. Unmanaged cloud usage can lead to surprising bills with hidden costs like idle resources and underutilized services.

Wasted Resources: Many businesses unknowingly pay for resources they don't fully utilize, leading to wasted expenditure. This is like having a warehouse full of seasonal items you only need for a few months a year.

Stifled Innovation: Unnecessary cloud spending can limit your budget for exploring new technologies and innovative cloud solutions. This can restrict your ability to adapt and compete in the ever-evolving digital landscape.

Strategies for Cloud Cost Optimization:

Rightsizing Resources: Choose the most appropriate cloud resource type (e.g., virtual machine size) based on your actual workload requirements. This is like selecting the optimal storage containers for your inventory, ensuring they're not too big or too small.

Reserved Instances: Commit to purchasing cloud resources for a specific timeframe at a discounted rate if your usage is predictable. Think of it as negotiating bulk discounts with your suppliers for frequently used inventory items.

Spot Instances: Utilize unused cloud capacity offered at significantly lower prices, but be prepared for potential interruptions. This is like taking advantage of seasonal sales or clearance events to get good deals on inventory, but knowing those items might be limited in availability.

Automated Shutdown: Schedule non-critical resources to automatically power down during off-peak hours. Imagine closing down sections of your warehouse during slow business periods to save on electricity costs.

Cost Monitoring and Reporting: Leverage cloud provider tools to gain insights into your cloud spending and identify areas for optimization. Regular inventory checks are crucial for any business – cloud cost monitoring allows you to identify underutilized or unnecessary resources in your cloud environment.

Cloud Cost Management Tools: Utilize specialized tools that provide detailed cost breakdowns, anomaly detection, and automated optimization recommendations. Imagine having sophisticated inventory management software that tracks usage patterns, identifies slow-moving items, and suggests ways to optimize your stock levels.

Benefits of Cloud Cost Optimization:

- **Reduced Cloud Spending:** Pay only for the resources you use, leading to significant cost savings.
- **Improved Profitability:** Free up resources to invest in other areas of your business and boost your bottom line.
- **Enhanced Efficiency:** Optimize resource allocation and ensure you're getting the most out of your cloud investment.
- **Increased Agility:** Free up budget for exploring new cloud solutions and experimenting with innovative technologies.

Cloud cost optimization is not a one-time fix; it's an ongoing process. By adopting these strategies and monitoring your cloud spending habits, you can ensure your cloud environment is lean and efficient.

Remember, a well-managed cloud environment is like a well-stocked warehouse – you have the resources you need to thrive, without the burden of unnecessary costs. This allows you to focus on growing your business and achieving your strategic goals.

CLOUD EXPLORATION

1. The cloud computing landscape is a vast and ever-evolving realm, offering a multitude of benefits for businesses of all sizes. It serves as a digital buffet, brimming with on-demand resources, scalable storage, and powerful applications. Unlike traditional on-premise IT infrastructure, the cloud eliminates the need for upfront hardware investments and complex maintenance. This translates to lower costs and increased agility, allowing businesses to adapt to changing needs with ease.

Exploration of the cloud opens doors to a world of possibilities. From deploying cutting-edge artificial intelligence tools to leveraging serverless computing for efficient task execution, the cloud empowers businesses to innovate and gain a competitive edge. Additionally, robust security features and disaster recovery solutions ensure your valuable data remains protected. Whether you're a budding startup or a well-established enterprise, embarking on a cloud exploration journey can unlock a treasure trove of potential, paving the way for a more efficient, scalable, and secure digital future.

UNDERSTANDING CLOUD BENEFITS

Cloud computing offers a similar abundance of benefits for businesses of all sizes. By migrating to the cloud, you gain access to a wealth of resources and capabilities that can transform your operations and empower your organization for success. Let's delve into the key advantages that cloud computing brings to the table:

Enhanced Agility and Scalability: The cloud eliminates the limitations of fixed infrastructure. You can dynamically scale resources up or down on-demand, adapting to fluctuating workloads and business needs. This agility is like having a team that can quickly adjust its size and skillset based on project requirements.

Reduced Costs: Cloud computing offers a pay-as-you-go model, eliminating the upfront investment required for traditional on-premise IT infrastructure. You only pay for the resources you use, optimizing your spending and freeing up capital for other strategic investments. Think of it as buying fresh produce only when you need it, instead of having a large, expensive on-site garden to maintain.

Improved Accessibility and Collaboration: Cloud-based applications and data are accessible from anywhere with an internet connection. This fosters remote work opportunities, enhances collaboration across teams and locations, and empowers a more flexible work environment. Imagine a team being able to access and work on the same documents simultaneously, regardless of their physical location.

Increased Security and Reliability: Cloud providers invest heavily in robust security measures and disaster recovery solutions. Your data resides in secure data centers, protected from physical threats and cyberattacks. Additionally, cloud services offer high availability, ensuring minimal downtime and business continuity. This translates to peace of mind, knowing your valuable data is safeguarded and your applications are always accessible.

Automatic Updates and Maintenance: Cloud providers handle software updates and infrastructure maintenance, freeing up your IT team to focus on more strategic initiatives. Imagine never having to worry about manually patching and updating your computer software – the cloud takes care of it for you.

Access to Cutting-Edge Technologies: Cloud computing provides access to a vast array of innovative technologies, including artificial intelligence, machine learning, and big data analytics. These tools can be leveraged to gain valuable insights, automate tasks, and drive business growth. This is like having access to the latest farming tools and techniques to maximize your harvest and stay ahead of the curve.

Understanding these benefits empowers you to make informed decisions about cloud adoption. By carefully considering your specific business needs and selecting the right cloud services, you can unlock the full potential of the cloud and cultivate a thriving digital landscape for your organization. Remember, the cloud isn't just a technological marvel; it's a strategic tool that can help you achieve your business goals and gain a competitive edge in today's dynamic market.

CLOUD ADOPTION STRATEGIES

Transitioning your business to the cloud is an exciting journey, but navigating the vast landscape can seem daunting. Here, we'll explore various cloud adoption strategies to help you chart a course towards a successful cloud migration:

1. Define Your Goals and Needs:

Business Objectives: Clearly articulate your business goals for cloud adoption. Are you seeking cost reduction, improved scalability, or access to new technologies? Knowing your "why" is crucial for making informed decisions.

Workload Assessment: Evaluate your current IT infrastructure and workloads. Not all applications are ideal candidates for the cloud. Identify the workloads that will benefit most from cloud migration.

2. Choose the Right Cloud Model:

Deployment Models: Select the deployment model that aligns with your security and control requirements. Public cloud offers the most flexibility and scalability, while private cloud provides a dedicated environment for sensitive data. Hybrid cloud combines both for a tailored solution.

Service Models: Choose the service model that best suits your needs. Infrastructure as a Service (IaaS) offers full control over virtual machines, Platform as a Service (PaaS) provides a platform for application development, and Software as a Service (SaaS) delivers ready-to-use applications.

3. Develop a Migration Plan:

Phased Approach: Consider a phased migration approach, starting with non-critical workloads and gradually moving to more complex applications. This minimizes disruption and allows you to learn and adapt throughout the process.

Cost Optimization: Factor in cloud service costs and potential savings. Utilize tools and strategies like reserved instances or spot instances to optimize your cloud spending.

4. Security and Compliance:

Data Security: Prioritize data security by implementing robust access controls and encryption measures. Ensure your chosen cloud provider adheres to relevant industry regulations and compliance standards.

Disaster Recovery: Establish a comprehensive disaster recovery plan to ensure business continuity in case of unforeseen events. Leverage cloud-based backup and recovery solutions for added protection.

5. Change Management and Training:

Employee Buy-in: Foster employee buy-in by communicating the benefits of cloud adoption and providing adequate training on new cloud-based tools and processes. A well-informed and prepared workforce is essential for a smooth transition.

6. Continuous Monitoring and Optimization:

Performance Monitoring: Continuously monitor your cloud environment to identify potential bottlenecks and optimize resource utilization. Cloud platforms offer tools for detailed performance analysis.

Cost Management: Regularly review your cloud spending and identify areas for further cost optimization. Utilize cloud cost management tools for automated monitoring and recommendations.

By following these cloud adoption strategies, you can embark on a successful cloud migration journey. Remember, cloud adoption is not a one-time event; it's an ongoing process. Continuous monitoring, optimization, and adaptation will ensure your cloud environment remains aligned with your evolving business needs. With a well-defined strategy and a focus on these key considerations, you can harness the transformative power of the cloud and propel your business towards a thriving digital future.

CLOUD READINESS ASSESSMENT

Imagine planning a trip to a new country. Before packing your bags and booking flights, you'd likely assess your readiness – checking visa requirements, researching local customs, and learning basic phrases. A cloud readiness assessment serves a similar purpose for businesses considering cloud adoption. It's a comprehensive evaluation process that helps you determine your organization's preparedness for migrating to the cloud.

Conduct a Cloud Readiness Assessment

- **Identify Strengths and Weaknesses:** Uncover areas where your current IT infrastructure is efficient and highlight potential challenges that might arise during cloud migration.
- **Define Migration Strategy:** The assessment results provide a roadmap for developing a tailored cloud adoption strategy that considers your specific needs and limitations.
- **Minimize Risks and Disruptions:** By proactively identifying potential roadblocks, you can mitigate risks and minimize disruptions to your business operations during the migration process.
- **Cost Optimization:** A thorough assessment helps you optimize your cloud spending by pinpointing workloads that are well-suited for the cloud and identifying areas where cost-saving opportunities exist.
- **Enhanced Security Posture:** The assessment process helps evaluate your current security practices and ensures a secure transition to the cloud environment.

Key Areas Covered in a Cloud Readiness Assessment:

Business Objectives: Understanding your business goals for cloud adoption is crucial for tailoring the migration strategy and measuring success.

IT Infrastructure Assessment: Evaluate your current IT infrastructure, including hardware, software, applications, and data storage. Identify workloads that are most suitable for cloud migration.

Security and Compliance: Analyze your security policies and compliance requirements to ensure a smooth transition to a secure cloud environment.

Network Connectivity: Assess your network bandwidth and connectivity to determine if it can handle the demands of cloud-based applications and data transfer.

People and Skills: Evaluate your IT team's skills and knowledge to identify any training needs before migrating to the cloud.

Benefits of Conducting a Cloud Readiness Assessment:

- **Informed Decision-Making:** The assessment provides valuable insights to help you make informed decisions about cloud adoption, ensuring a smooth and successful migration.
- **Reduced Risks:** By proactively identifying potential challenges, you can mitigate risks and minimize disruptions to your business operations.
- **Improved Cloud ROI:** A well-defined cloud adoption strategy ensures you leverage the cloud's capabilities effectively, maximizing your return on investment.
- **Enhanced Agility and Scalability:** The cloud readiness assessment helps you lay the groundwork for a more agile and scalable IT infrastructure to support future business growth.

Conducting a cloud readiness assessment is an essential first step towards a successful cloud migration journey. By investing in this assessment, you gain valuable insights that empower you to make informed decisions, minimize risks, and unlock the full potential of the cloud for your organization. Remember, a well-prepared traveler has a smoother journey, and the same principle applies to cloud adoption. With a thorough cloud readiness assessment, you can confidently embark on your cloud migration adventure and navigate towards a thriving digital future.

CLOUD MIGRATION

Cloud migration is the process of moving your data, applications, and IT resources from on-premise servers to a cloud environment. Imagine relocating your business operations from a physical office to a virtual workspace in the cloud. This transition offers several advantages, including increased scalability and agility – you can easily adjust your resources up or down as needed. Additionally, cloud migration can lead to cost savings as you only pay for the resources you use, eliminating the need for upfront hardware investments and ongoing maintenance. However, migrating to the cloud requires careful planning and execution. A cloud readiness assessment can help you evaluate your organization's preparedness and develop a tailored migration strategy. By following a well-defined plan and considering factors like security and network connectivity, you can ensure a smooth and successful transition to the cloud, paving the way for a more efficient and scalable digital future for your business.

PLANNING CLOUD MIGRATION

Migrating your business to the cloud is like launching a rocket – exciting, potentially transformative, but requiring careful planning and execution. A well-defined cloud migration plan acts as your launchpad, ensuring a smooth and successful journey to the cloud. Here's a breakdown of the key steps involved in planning your cloud migration:

Define Your Goals and Needs:

Clearly articulate your goals for cloud adoption. Are you seeking cost reduction, improved scalability, or access to innovative cloud-based technologies? Having a clear understanding of your "why" helps you prioritize tasks and make informed decisions throughout the migration process.

Evaluate your current IT infrastructure and applications. Not all applications are ideal candidates for the cloud. Identify the workloads that will benefit most from migration, considering factors like security requirements, processing needs, and integration complexity.

Choose Your Cloud Strategy:

Select the cloud deployment model that aligns with your security and control requirements. Public cloud offers the most flexibility and scalability, while private cloud provides a dedicated environment for sensitive data. Hybrid cloud combines both for a tailored solution.

Decide on the service model that best suits your needs. Infrastructure as a Service (IaaS) offers full control over virtual machines, Platform as a Service (PaaS) provides a platform for application development, and Software as a Service (SaaS) delivers ready-to-use applications.

Develop a Migration Plan:

Consider a phased migration approach, starting with non-critical workloads and gradually moving to more complex applications. This minimizes disruption and allows you to learn and adapt throughout the process. Imagine test-firing your rocket engine before launch!

Factor in cloud service costs and potential savings. Utilize tools and strategies like reserved instances or spot instances to optimize your cloud spending during migration and beyond.

Security and Compliance:

Prioritize data security by implementing robust access controls and encryption measures during the migration process. Ensure your chosen cloud provider adheres to relevant industry regulations and compliance standards. Data security is paramount, just like ensuring the structural integrity of your rocket!

Establish a comprehensive disaster recovery plan to ensure business continuity in case of unforeseen events. Leverage cloud-based backup and recovery solutions for added protection. Have a backup plan in place, in case of unexpected issues during launch.

Change Management and Training:

Foster employee buy-in by communicating the benefits of cloud adoption and providing adequate training on new cloud-based tools and processes. A well-informed and prepared workforce is essential for a smooth liftoff.

Identify any skill gaps within your IT team and provide training opportunities to ensure they possess the necessary expertise to manage the cloud environment effectively. Train your crew to operate the new launch controls!

Continual Monitoring and Optimization:

Continuously monitor your cloud environment after migration to identify potential bottlenecks and optimize resource utilization. Cloud platforms offer tools for detailed performance analysis. Track your rocket's trajectory and make adjustments as needed for a successful journey.

Regularly review your cloud spending and identify areas for further cost optimization. Utilize cloud cost management tools for automated monitoring and recommendations. Ensure you're using fuel efficiently throughout your cloud voyage.

Develop a comprehensive cloud migration plan that sets your organization on course for a successful launch into the cloud. Remember, planning is crucial for a smooth and secure migration. With a well-defined plan in place, you can leverage the transformative power of the cloud and propel your business towards a thriving digital future.

CLOUD MIGRATION TOOLS AND TECHNIQUES

Exploration of the essential tools and techniques that will equip your team for a successful cloud migration:

Cloud Migration Tools:

Assessment Tools: Cloud readiness assessment tools help evaluate your current IT infrastructure and identify workloads best suited for the cloud. These tools act as your compass, guiding you towards a smooth migration path.

Data Migration Tools: These tools facilitate the secure and efficient transfer of your data to the cloud environment. Imagine having specialized packing crates to ensure your data arrives safely at its new home.

Cloud Management Platforms (CMPs): CMPs provide a centralized console for managing and monitoring your cloud resources. Think of them as the captain's bridge, offering a comprehensive view of your cloud migration and ongoing operations.

Cloud Security Tools: Cloud security tools help safeguard your data and applications during and after migration. These tools are your life vests, ensuring the security of your valuable assets throughout the journey.

Cloud Migration Techniques:

Lift and Shift: This simplest approach involves migrating existing applications and data "as-is" to the cloud.

It's a quick way to move to the cloud, but may not leverage the full potential of cloud capabilities. Imagine transporting your entire office furniture directly to the new location, without considering potential space optimizations.

Refactoring/Replatforming: This technique involves optimizing applications to benefit from cloud-native features like scalability and elasticity. Think of renovating your office furniture to better suit the new workspace layout.

Hybrid Cloud: This approach combines on-premise infrastructure with the cloud, offering a flexible solution for workloads with specific security or compliance requirements. Imagine having a hybrid work model, with some employees working remotely (cloud) and others working from the office (on-premise).

Cloud-Native Development: This approach involves building applications specifically for the cloud environment, leveraging its unique features and functionalities from the ground up. Think of designing and building furniture specifically for your new office space, maximizing its functionality and aesthetics.

By selecting the right combination of tools and techniques, you can tailor your cloud migration strategy to your specific needs. Remember, there's no one-size-fits-all approach. The best tools and techniques depend on the complexity of your IT environment, your desired outcomes, and your organization's risk tolerance.

Additional Considerations:

- **Testing and Validation:** Thoroughly test migrated applications and data to ensure they function correctly in the cloud environment. Conducting test runs is crucial before officially launching your new office space.

- **Change Management:** Effectively communicate the migration process to your employees and provide training on new cloud-based tools and processes. Keeping your crew informed and prepared ensures a smooth transition.

With the right tools, techniques, and planning, your cloud migration can be a successful voyage, propelling your business towards a more efficient and scalable digital future. Remember, a well-equipped crew and a well-defined course are essential for a successful journey, and cloud migration is no exception.

CHAPTER ELEVEN

CLOUD TRANSFORMATION

Cloud transformation is a comprehensive journey that transcends simply migrating data and applications to the cloud. It's a strategic shift that reimagines how your business operates, leverages technology, and fosters innovation. This transformation unlocks the full potential of cloud computing, empowering your organization with agility, scalability, and cost-effectiveness. At the heart of cloud transformation lies a cultural shift. It's about moving away from rigid, on-premise infrastructure and embracing a more dynamic and adaptable approach. Cloud technology empowers you to scale resources up or down on-demand, seamlessly adjusting to fluctuating workloads and business needs. Imagine having a team that can effortlessly adjust its size and skillset based on project requirements – that's the agility cloud transformation brings. Cost optimization is another key driver of cloud transformation. The cloud eliminates the need for upfront hardware investments and complex maintenance, often resulting in significant cost savings. You only pay for the resources you use, freeing up capital for other strategic initiatives. Think of it like switching from owning a fleet of vehicles to a ride-sharing service – you only pay for the transportation you need, when you need it. Cloud transformation also opens doors to a world of innovative technologies. Artificial intelligence, machine learning, and big data analytics become readily available, empowering you to gain valuable insights from your data, automate tasks, and drive business growth. It's like having access to cutting-edge tools and techniques that can revolutionize the way you operate. Security remains paramount throughout cloud transformation. Cloud providers invest heavily in robust security measures and disaster recovery solutions to safeguard your valuable data. Regular updates, automatic backups, and encryption protocols ensure your information remains protected, even in the face of unforeseen events. Imagine having a state-of-the-art security system for your data center, providing peace of mind and business continuity.

Cloud transformation is not a one-time event; it's an ongoing process of optimization and adaptation. By continuously monitoring your cloud environment, identifying areas for improvement, and embracing new technologies, you can ensure your organization stays ahead of the curve. It's like regularly maintaining your office space and equipment to ensure it continues to function optimally. Ultimately, cloud transformation is a journey towards a more efficient, scalable, and secure digital future. By embarking on this journey, you empower your organization to thrive in today's dynamic and ever-evolving business landscape.

MODERNIZING APPLICATION FOR THE CLOUD

Modernizing applications for the cloud follows a similar principle. It's the process of updating and optimizing your existing applications to thrive in the cloud environment. This transformation unlocks a multitude of benefits, propelling your business towards a more efficient and scalable digital future.

Modernize Applications for the Cloud

Enhanced Performance and Scalability: Cloud-based applications can leverage the on-demand resources of the cloud, scaling up or down to meet fluctuating workloads. This translates to faster processing times, improved responsiveness, and the ability to handle unexpected surges in traffic. Think of having more meeting rooms and flexible workspaces to accommodate a growing team, ensuring everyone has the space they need to be productive.

Increased Agility and Innovation: Modernized cloud applications are easier to deploy, update, and manage. This agility allows you to adapt to changing market conditions and rapidly implement new features, fostering a culture of innovation within your organization. Imagine having modular furniture that can be easily rearranged to adapt to new project requirements or team structures.

Reduced Costs: By eliminating the need for expensive on-premise infrastructure and software licenses, cloud modernization can lead to significant cost savings. Additionally, cloud-based applications often benefit from automated maintenance and updates, freeing up your IT team to focus on strategic initiatives. Think of downsizing from a large office building to a more efficient co-working space, reducing overhead costs and allowing you to invest in new technologies.

Improved Security and Reliability: Cloud providers invest heavily in robust security measures and disaster recovery solutions. Modernized cloud applications benefit from these advanced security features, ensuring your data remains protected and your applications are always accessible. Imagine upgrading your office security system and implementing automated backups to safeguard your equipment and critical documents.

Key Strategies for Application Modernization:

Lift and Shift: This simplest approach involves migrating existing applications "as-is" to the cloud. While it offers a quick migration path, it may not fully leverage the cloud's capabilities. Think of moving your existing furniture to the new office space without considering potential layout optimizations.

Refactoring/Replatforming: This strategy involves optimizing applications to benefit from cloud-native features like microservices and containers. This approach unlocks the full potential of the cloud for improved performance and scalability. Imagine revamping your furniture and utilizing space-saving solutions to create a more efficient and functional workspace.

Cloud-Native Development: This approach involves building entirely new applications specifically designed for the cloud environment, leveraging its unique features and functionalities from the ground up. Think of designing and building custom furniture that perfectly fits the new office space and maximizes its functionality

The Right Approach for Your Needs:

The optimal modernization strategy depends on the complexity of your applications, your desired outcomes, and your organization's budget. A thorough assessment can help you determine the most suitable approach for your specific needs.

Modernizing applications for the cloud is a strategic investment. By embracing this transformation, you can empower your business with agility, scalability, and cost-effectiveness, paving the way for a thriving digital future. Remember, a modern and well-equipped office fosters a productive and innovative work environment – the same principle applies to your cloud applications.

CLOUD-BASED BUSINESS MODELS

Hybrid Cloud Model:

This model combines two or more cloud deployment models (e.g., IaaS and SaaS) or a mix of on-premise infrastructure and cloud services. It allows businesses to tailor their cloud usage based on specific needs.The hybrid cloud model offers flexibility, security, and control. Businesses can leverage the benefits of the cloud for specific workloads while keeping sensitive data on-premise.

Cloud-Based Marketplaces:

These online platforms connect businesses that offer cloud-based services with potential customers. They function similarly to traditional marketplaces, but focus on cloud services and software solutions.

Examples: Popular examples include Salesforce AppExchange and Shopify App Store, which offer a vast array of cloud-based applications for businesses of all sizes.Cloud marketplaces provide businesses with easy access to a wide range of cloud-based solutions and tools, fostering innovation and competition within the cloud ecosystem.

Choosing the Right Cloud-Based Business Model:

The optimal model depends on several factors, including your target market, the type of service you offer, and your desired level of control. Carefully evaluate your business needs and cloud offerings before selecting the model that best aligns with your strategy.

Cloud-based business models are transforming the way businesses operate. By embracing these innovative models, you can unlock new revenue streams, improve efficiency, and gain a competitive edge in the dynamic digital landscape. Remember, the cloud is not just a technological advancement; it's a strategic opportunity to redefine your business and propel it towards a thriving future.

• 91 •

CHAPTER TWELVE

CLOUD MASTERY

In the ever-evolving realm of cloud computing, achieving Cloud Mastery is akin to scaling Mount Everest. It's a challenging but rewarding pursuit that equips you with the knowledge and skills to navigate the complex landscape and unlock the full potential of the cloud for your organization. Mastery goes beyond simply understanding how to use cloud services. It's about developing a strategic mindset, optimizing cloud resource allocation, and ensuring cost-effectiveness. A Cloud Master can identify the most suitable cloud deployment model (public, private, or hybrid) for specific workloads, leverage automation tools to streamline processes, and implement robust security measures to safeguard sensitive data. The path to Cloud Mastery is paved with continuous learning. New technologies and best practices emerge constantly, requiring cloud professionals to stay updated and adapt their skillsets. This journey often involves pursuing cloud certifications offered by major providers like AWS, Microsoft Azure, and Google Cloud Platform. These certifications validate your expertise and demonstrate your commitment to excellence in the cloud domain. Cloud Mastery isn't just about individual brilliance; it's about fostering a culture of cloud competency within your organization. By empowering your team with the necessary knowledge and skills, you can create a collaborative environment that maximizes the benefits of cloud adoption. This collaborative approach ensures everyone is on the same page, enabling your organization to leverage the cloud effectively and propel itself towards a more efficient, scalable, and secure digital future. Ultimately, Cloud Mastery is not a destination, but rather a continuous voyage of exploration and optimization. By embracing this pursuit, you position yourself and your organization to thrive in the dynamic world of cloud computing.

CLOUD GOVERNANCE

The cloud with a treasure trove of resources and endless possibilities. Cloud governance acts as your compass and rudder, ensuring your organization charts a safe, efficient, and successful course on this digital voyage. It's a framework of policies, processes, and controls that guide how your team utilizes cloud services to achieve your business goals.

Cloud Governance Essential?

Cloud governance helps you avoid cloud sprawl – the uncontrolled proliferation of unused or underutilized cloud resources. By implementing cost management strategies and monitoring resource allocation, you can optimize your cloud spending and maximize your return on investment (ROI).

Cloud governance establishes robust security measures to protect your sensitive data in the cloud. This includes setting access controls, data encryption protocols, and incident response plans to ensure compliance with relevant industry regulations.

Effective cloud governance facilitates a culture of innovation and experimentation within the cloud environment. By streamlining workflows and establishing clear approval processes for new cloud resources, your team can adapt and scale more efficiently to meet changing business needs.

Cloud governance helps mitigate risks associated with cloud adoption. This includes establishing clear roles and responsibilities for cloud resource management, preventing unauthorized access, and minimizing configuration errors that could disrupt operations.

Key Components of Cloud Governance:

- **Strategic Alignment:** Ensure your cloud governance framework aligns with your overall business strategy and IT objectives.
- **Security and Compliance:** Implement robust security measures and establish processes to adhere to relevant industry regulations.
- **Cost Management:** Develop strategies to optimize cloud spending and monitor resource allocation.
- **Performance Management:** Continuously monitor your cloud environment to identify areas for optimization and ensure efficient resource utilization.
- **Change Management:** Effectively communicate cloud governance policies and procedures to all stakeholders within your organization.

Benefits of Implementing Cloud Governance:

- **Increased Efficiency and Productivity:** Clear policies and streamlined workflows enable your team to utilize cloud resources effectively and focus on core business activities.

- **Reduced Risks and Errors:** Cloud governance minimizes security breaches, configuration errors, and unauthorized access, safeguarding your data and ensuring business continuity.
- **Improved Decision-Making:** Data-driven insights gained through cloud governance enable informed decision-making regarding cloud resource allocation and cost optimization strategies.
- **Enhanced Innovation:** A well-defined cloud governance framework fosters a culture of innovation by encouraging experimentation and secure exploration of new technologies within the cloud environment.

Cloud governance is not a one-time event; it's an ongoing process. Regularly review and update your cloud governance framework to adapt to evolving security threats, new cloud technologies, and your organization's changing needs. By prioritizing cloud governance, you empower your organization to harness the full potential of the cloud and navigate your digital journey with confidence and clarity.

CLOUD CENTRE OF EXCELLENCE

A seasoned guide, equipped with knowledge, resources, and a strategic plan, would be invaluable. In the realm of cloud computing, a Cloud Center of Excellence (CCoE) fulfills a similar role. It's a dedicated team that acts as your central hub for guiding and accelerating your organization's successful cloud adoption and ongoing optimization.

The Core Functions of a Cloud Center of Excellence:

Strategy and Planning: The CCoE plays a pivotal role in defining your cloud strategy. This includes assessing your IT infrastructure, identifying suitable cloud adoption models, and developing a roadmap for migration and ongoing management.

Governance and Compliance: The CCoE establishes and enforces cloud governance policies that ensure security, compliance, and cost-effectiveness throughout your cloud journey. This includes setting access controls, data encryption protocols, and implementing processes to adhere to relevant industry regulations.

Education and Training: The CCoE empowers your workforce by providing training and knowledge sharing opportunities on cloud technologies, best practices, and security protocols. This ensures a smooth transition for your employees and fosters a culture of cloud literacy within your organization.

Standardization and Optimization: The CCoE promotes the adoption of standardized cloud tools and configurations, streamlining cloud resource management and facilitating ongoing optimization. This helps eliminate inefficiencies and ensures you leverage the cloud's full potential.

Cloud Adoption Advocacy: The CCoE champions the benefits of cloud adoption across your organization. By fostering collaboration and addressing concerns, they encourage widespread cloud usage and alignment with your overall business goals.

Benefits of Establishing a Cloud Center of Excellence:

- **Accelerated Cloud Adoption:** The CCoE provides a centralized resource for knowledge, best practices, and guidance, enabling your organization to adopt the cloud faster and more efficiently.
- **Enhanced Security and Compliance:** Robust cloud governance practices implemented by the CCoE safeguard your sensitive data and ensure adherence to

industry regulations.

- **Reduced Costs:** Through standardization and optimization strategies, the CCoE helps you minimize cloud sprawl and optimize cloud resource allocation, leading to significant cost savings.
- **Improved Agility and Scalability:** The CCoE fosters a culture of innovation within the cloud environment. By streamlining approval processes and promoting best practices, they empower your teams to adapt and scale more efficiently.
- **Empowered Workforce:** A cloud-literate workforce equipped with the necessary skills to navigate the cloud environment is essential for successful cloud adoption. The CCoE plays a crucial role in developing this critical competency within your organization.

The Composition of a Cloud Center of Excellence:

The ideal structure of a CCoE can vary depending on your organization's size and cloud adoption goals. However, it typically consists of individuals with expertise in cloud technologies, governance, security, architecture, and training.

Cloud adoption is a transformative journey. By establishing a Cloud Center of Excellence, you equip yourself with a valuable guiding force. The CCoE empowers your organization to navigate the complexities of the cloud with greater confidence, security, and efficiency, ultimately propelling you towards a thriving digital future.

CLOUD INNOVATION

The cloud isn't just about storing data and running applications; it's a springboard for innovation. Imagine a vast, open sky – the cloud – where ideas can soar and transform into groundbreaking solutions. Cloud innovation unlocks a multitude of possibilities, empowering businesses to develop new products, improve existing services, and gain a competitive edge in the ever-evolving digital landscape.

Fueling Innovation with Cloud Capabilities:

Scalability and Agility: The cloud's on-demand nature allows businesses to scale resources up or down quickly. This agility fosters experimentation and rapid prototyping, enabling businesses to test and refine new ideas efficiently.

Cost-Effectiveness: Cloud eliminates the need for upfront hardware investments and complex maintenance. This frees up capital to invest in innovative projects and explore emerging technologies.

Access to Cutting-Edge Tools: Cloud platforms offer a vast array of innovative services like artificial intelligence (AI), machine learning (ML), and big data analytics. These tools empower businesses to extract valuable insights from data, automate tasks, and develop intelligent solutions.

Global Collaboration: The cloud fosters seamless collaboration across geographical boundaries. Teams can work together on projects in real-time, regardless of location, accelerating innovation cycles.

Examples of Cloud-Fueled Innovation:

Personalized Customer Experiences: Businesses can leverage cloud-based analytics to understand customer behavior and preferences, enabling them to personalize marketing campaigns and product recommendations.

Revolutionizing Healthcare: Cloud platforms facilitate secure storage and analysis of medical data, leading to advancements in remote patient monitoring, drug discovery, and personalized medicine.

Transforming Manufacturing: The cloud empowers manufacturers to implement AI-powered predictive maintenance and optimize production lines, leading to increased efficiency and reduced downtime.

Strategies for Fostering Cloud Innovation:

- **Culture of Experimentation:** Encourage a culture that embraces experimentation and calculated risks. Provide resources and support for employees to explore new ideas and develop innovative solutions using the cloud.
- **Invest in Skills Development:** Equip your workforce with the necessary skills to leverage cloud-based tools and technologies effectively. This includes training on data analysis, AI, and cloud architecture.
- **Embrace a "Fail Fast, Learn Faster" Mentality:** Recognize that not all experiments will succeed. Encourage teams to learn from failures and iterate quickly to refine their ideas.
- **Partner with Cloud Providers:** Many cloud providers offer innovation programs and resources to support their customers. Leverage these resources to accelerate your innovation journey.

Cloud innovation is not a one-time event; it's an ongoing process. By continuously exploring new cloud capabilities, fostering a culture of creativity, and adapting to emerging trends, you can unlock the full potential of the cloud to drive sustainable innovation within your organization. As your business scales new heights in the digital sky, the cloud will remain your unwavering partner, propelling you towards a future brimming with groundbreaking possibilities.

CHAPTER THIRTEEN

CONCLUSION

In the ever-evolving culinary landscape of technology, the Cloud Cookbook emerges as an invaluable resource, offering a delectable spread of recipes for cloud success. Just as a skilled chef relies on a trusted cookbook to navigate complex dishes and create culinary masterpieces, this guide empowers you to approach cloud migration and optimization with confidence and a dash of ingenuity. Each recipe within the Cloud Cookbook serves as a meticulously crafted instruction manual, guiding you through the essential steps of cloud adoption. From assessing your IT infrastructure and selecting the most suitable cloud deployment model to implementing robust security measures and optimizing resource allocation, the cookbook equips you with the knowledge and practical steps to navigate the cloud kitchen with culinary finesse. But the Cloud Cookbook isn't merely a collection of static recipes; it's a dynamic and ever-evolving resource. As the cloud landscape continues to simmer with innovation, new recipes and techniques will undoubtedly emerge. By staying updated on the latest cloud trends and best practices, you can ensure your cloud cookbook remains a relevant and valuable companion on your digital culinary journey. The true power of the Cloud Cookbook, however, lies not just in the recipes themselves, but in fostering a culture of experimentation and continuous improvement within your organization. Imagine your team as a collaborative kitchen, where each member brings their unique skills and perspectives to the table. By embracing this collaborative spirit and encouraging innovation, you can leverage the Cloud Cookbook as a springboard for developing your own signature cloud recipes, perfectly tailored to your organization's specific needs and goals. Ultimately, the Cloud Cookbook is more than just a collection of recipes; it's a catalyst for transformation. By following its guidance and fostering a culture of cloud literacy within your organization, you can unlock the full potential of the cloud, propelling your business towards a future brimming with efficiency, agility, and innovation. So, grab your metaphorical apron, delve into the Cloud Cookbook, and embark on your own delicious journey towards cloud success!

The Cloud Cookbook offers a comprehensive menu for cloud success, but there's always room for a deeper dive or a delectable side dish to enhance your cloud culinary experience. Here arc some ways to expand your knowledge and expertise beyond the core recipes: Major cloud providers like AWS, Microsoft Azure, and Google Cloud Platform (GCP) each offer unique flavors and functionalities. Explore their documentation, tutorials, and certification programs to become a master chef in their specific cloud kitchens. The open-source cloud community is a treasure trove of innovative tools and libraries. Explore projects like OpenStack and Kubernetes to add versatility and customization to your cloud recipes. Cloud security is paramount. Delve deeper into security best practices, explore penetration testing methodologies, and stay updated on the latest cloud security threats to ensure your cloud dishes are firewalled against vulnerabilities.

Cloud cost management is an ongoing process. Explore cloud cost optimization tools, leverage reserved instances and spot pricing strategies, and continuously monitor your cloud spending to ensure you're getting the most out of your cloud investment. your cloud knowledge and learnings with your team. Conduct workshops, participate in cloud communities, and foster a culture of knowledge sharing within your organization to create a well-rounded team of cloud connoisseurs. By venturing beyond the core recipes and exploring these additional resources, you can transform the Cloud Cookbook into a dynamic and ever-evolving testament to your organization's cloud mastery. Remember, the cloud culinary landscape is vast and ever-changing. Embrace the spirit of exploration, experiment with new ingredients and techniques, and continuously refine your cloud recipes to ensure your organization remains at the forefront of digital innovation. With the Cloud Cookbook as your guide and a dash of creativity, you can create a winning formula for cloud success that will leave your competitors hungry for more.

CHAPTER FOURTEEN

ABOUT AUTHORS

Mr.A.Devendhiran, is currently working as a Assistant Professor in the department of Computer Science and Technnonogy at Vivekanandha College of Engineering for Women (Autonomous), Tiruchengode, Namakkal (D.t) Tamilnadu. He has 11 years 9 months of Teaching and industry experience. He has completed her B.Tech. (IT) degree from SSM College of Engineering, Namakkal, Tamilnadu and obtained her M.E degree (CSE) from St. Peter's University, Chennai, Tamilnadu. He has actively participated in workshops, and Seminars, Webinar and Faculty Development Program in both National and International levels. He has published 2 Scopus Index Journals paper and 1 Patent. Then 2 IEEE Conference paper published. His area of specialization includes Computer Networks, Artificial Intelligence, Cloud Computing. He has produced 100% results in UG.

Ms.L.Vishnu Priyais a dedicated professional with a passion for education. She holds a M.Tech degree in Information Technology and a B.E degree in Computer Science and Technology. she is currently working as an Assistant Professor at Vivekanandha College of Engineering for Women (Autonomous), Elayampalayam, Tiruchengode, Namakkal (Dt). She has actively participated in Faculty Development Program and also she has published one paper in the Conference and Published one paper journal. She is having interest in the research area of Deep Learning, Machine learning, Data Science, and Artificial Intelligence.

Ms.J.John Merina is a dedicated professional with a passion for education. She holds a M.Tech degree in Information Technology and a B.E degree in Information Technology. She was worked as online Tutor for 3 years and she is currently working as an Assistant Professor at Vivekanandha College of Engineering for Women (Autonomous), Elayampalayam, Tiruchengode, Namakkal (Dt). She has actively participated in Faculty Development Program and also she has published one paper in the Conference. She is having interest in the research area of Machine Learning, Data Science, and Artificial Intelligence.